Be Here Now Vieques

Michael Franco
mike@viequesguidebook.com

Be Here Now: Vieques
The Most Complete and Continuously Updated Guide Available

Copyright © 2008 by Michael Franco. All rights reserved. No part of this book may be reproduced or transmitted in any form or by any means, electronic or otherwise, including photocopying, recording, or by any information storage and retrieval system, without written permission from the author.

First Edition published 2008.

ISBN 1440442428
EAN-13 9781440442421
Library of Congress Control Number 008909706

Edited by Diane Curry

Cover design and maps by Tanty Indrus, Singapore

*For Diane, the woman who shapes the man
and the words he writes.*

*And for Porter, one hell of a jungle poodle
who taught me the importance of being here now.*

**This crazy rock has got a lot
of romance and sex appeal ...**

"Magic"
Kenny Chesney, *Be As You Are*

**I believe that down on the beach,
where the seagulls preach,
is where the Chinese buried the truth ...**

"Coastal Confessions"
Jimmy Buffet, *License To Chill*

A Note From the Author

It had been a dream of mine for years – chuck it all and head to the Caribbean a la a Jimmy Buffet song. In September of 2005, the dream became a reality as an employment opportunity dropped in the collective lap of myself and my wife, Diane. The draw to the tropics was so strong that we sold the bed and breakfast we had owned for four years in Pennsylvania Dutch country, packed our two-year old standard poodle and a few belongings and undertook a major change in latitude by moving to Vieques.

Like all jobs, ours had its share of difficulties – life on a tropical island wasn't exactly all coconuts and rum cocktails (although there were plenty of the latter). But whenever we got too wound-up or beaten-down, all it took to release a little stress and remember how truly fortunate we were was a trip to one of Vieques' blessedly beautiful beaches.

After two years, another job opportunity took us to Singapore where we currently live. Still, whenever life gets a little too crazy, the memory of those Vieques beaches is enough to blow my troubles away like a warm tropical breeze.

It is my hope that this guide helps you discover the same magic we did on Vieques. Like all guidebooks, this one is subjective, highlighting places I found interesting or unique in my time there. It is by no means exhaustive although I have done my best to offer a wide gamut of options for all travel tastes. As we still own property on Vieques and maintain contact with lots of island friends, you can feel confident that this book has been written by a true insider and is as current as possible.

That being said, **Be Here Now: Vieques** is produced through the modern wonder of Printing On Demand – meaning when you ordered it, a fresh copy was made just for you. Unlike other guidebooks, this one is updated constantly, sometimes on a daily basis! Therefore, if you find some inaccuracy or feel a particular property or site should be mentioned that isn't, please feel free to drop me a line at the email below. Likewise, if there's something you particularly enjoyed, I'd like to hear about that as well.

Here's wishing you long days, perfect weather, fine food, good company and sun-soaked memories to last a lifetime.

Michael Franco
mike@viequesguidebook.com

Página De Gracias

While I *love* islands, putting a book like this together made the point that – as the old expression states – no man *is* an island. Therefore, I'd like to extend my sincere gratitude to the following people who helped keep me in the (extra-loopy) island loop while I was putting together this book ...

Nugget

Vincent Tozzi

Aleks Janjic

Nancy Leslie

Kelly Thompson

Violet Ackas

Thomas Martin

JoAnne Hamilton

Karen Murphy

About The Maps

As my wife will say and, in fact, many wives will say about many husbands ... I'm not that good with directions. So, the maps in this book are meant to provide a general idea of island geography and the location of its various attractions, hotels and restaurants. For maps you can navigate by, I've decided to leave that part to the experts.

Pretty much the moment you land on the island, you will be able to score one of the excellent FREE maps put out either by Whizzbang Designs or Resort Maps. One or the other of them are available at virtually all of the hotels and car rental companies and better maps to the island simply can't be made. Should you wish to get oriented before you arrive, you can even view their maps online:

Whizzbang Designs
www.theviequesmap.com.
Be sure to click on different areas of the image for blown-up sections that show greater detail.

Resort Maps
www.resortmaps.com
Select Puerto Rico, then Vieques and click for a draggable, interactive map with advertiser information.

Of course, with an island the size of Vieques, you have to try <u>really hard</u> to get lost! It truly is simple to find your way around.

All that being said, when there is something particularly difficult to find (like the island's black sand beach), I have included written directions. And, don't worry, my wife approved them before they were allowed to leave my laptop!

Happy trails ...

Hotels

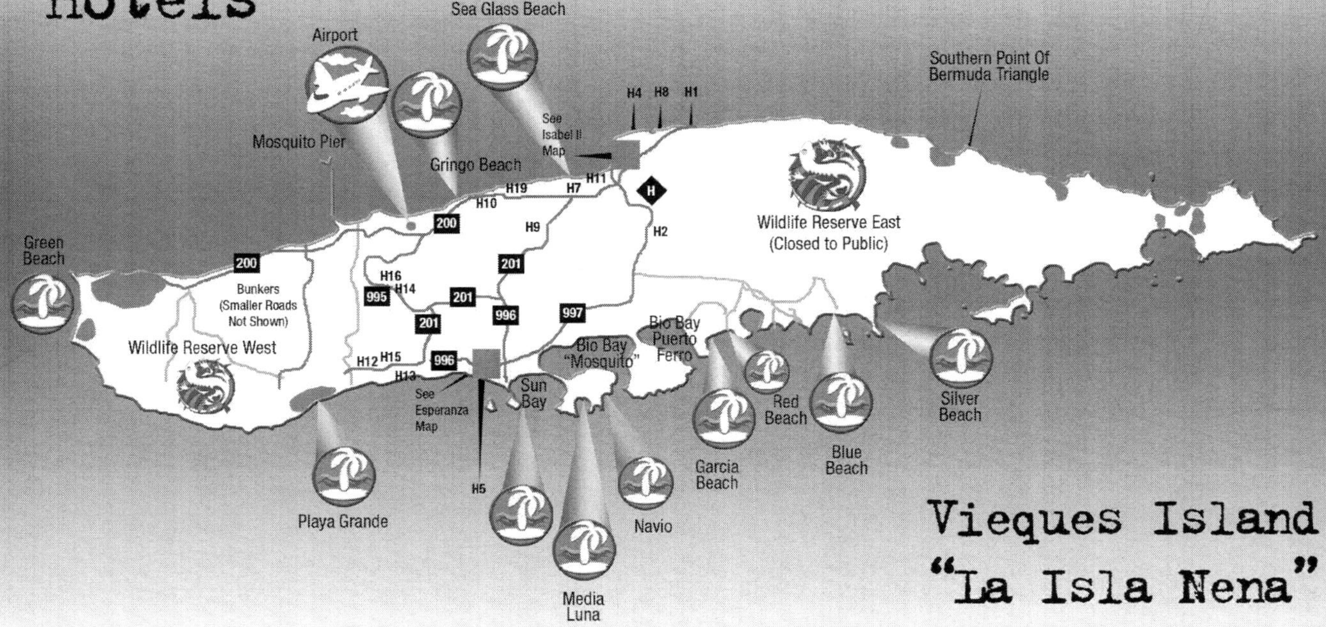

Vieques Island "La Isla Nena"

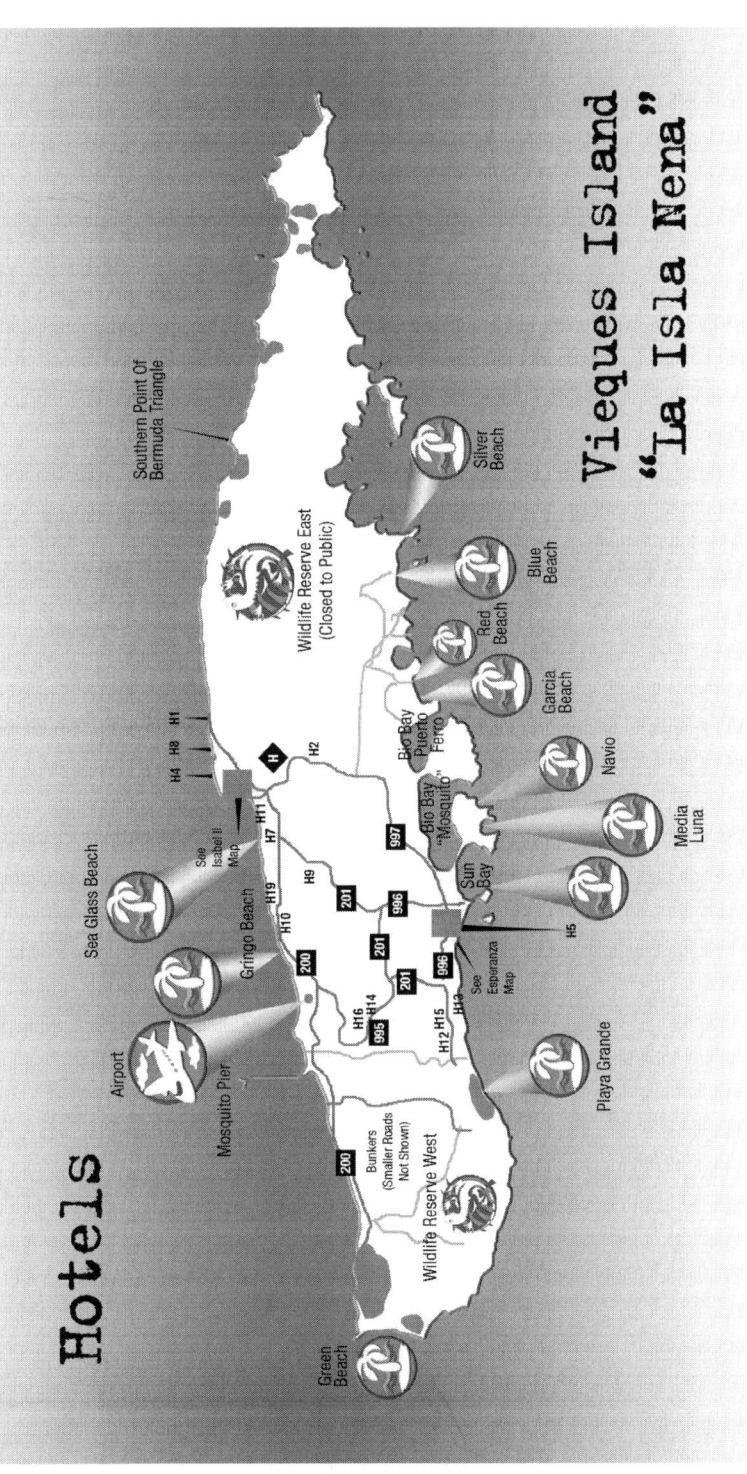

Restaurants and Shops

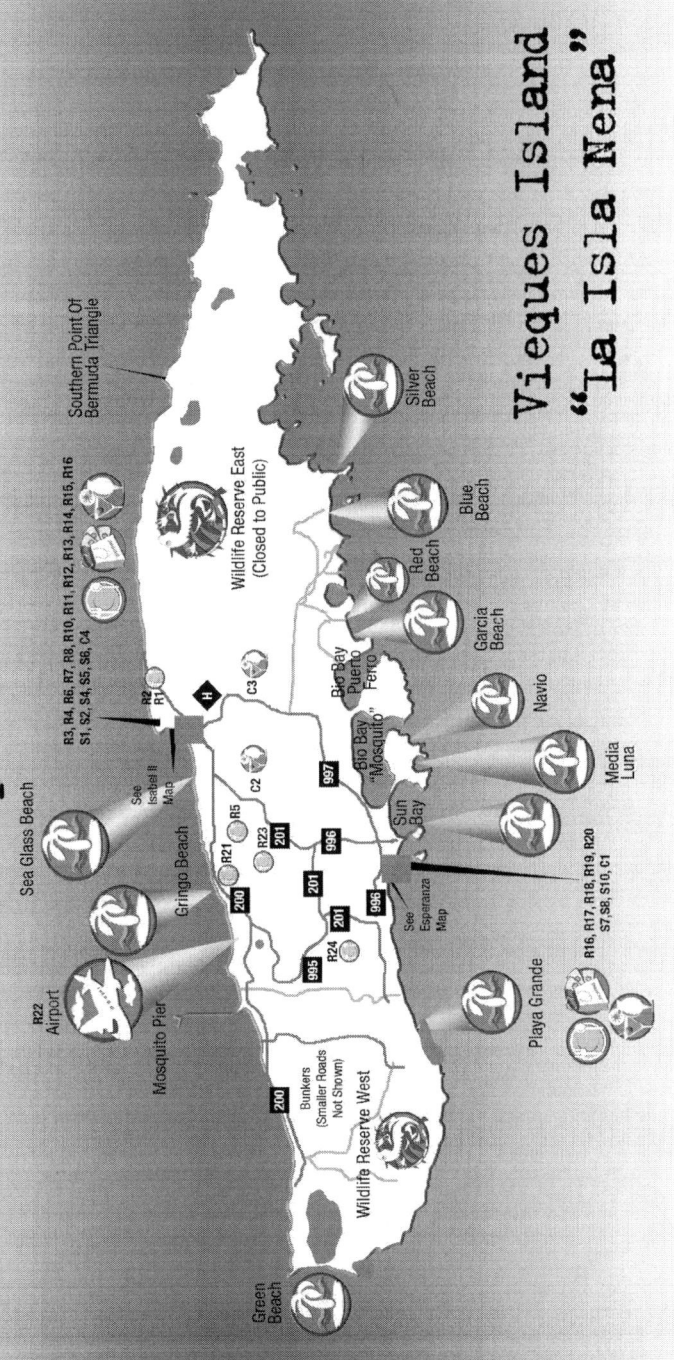

Vieques Island "La Isla Nena"

Isabel Segunda
Hotels, Restaurants and Shops

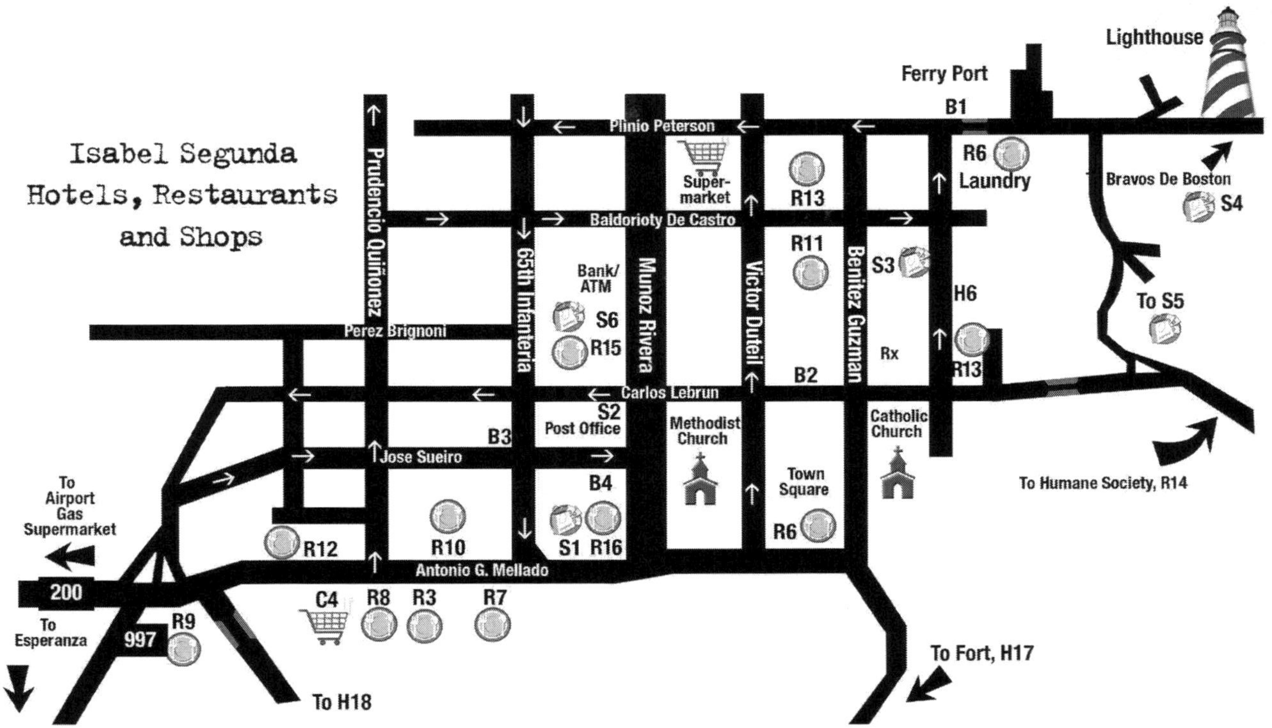

Esperanza Hotels, Restaurants and Shops

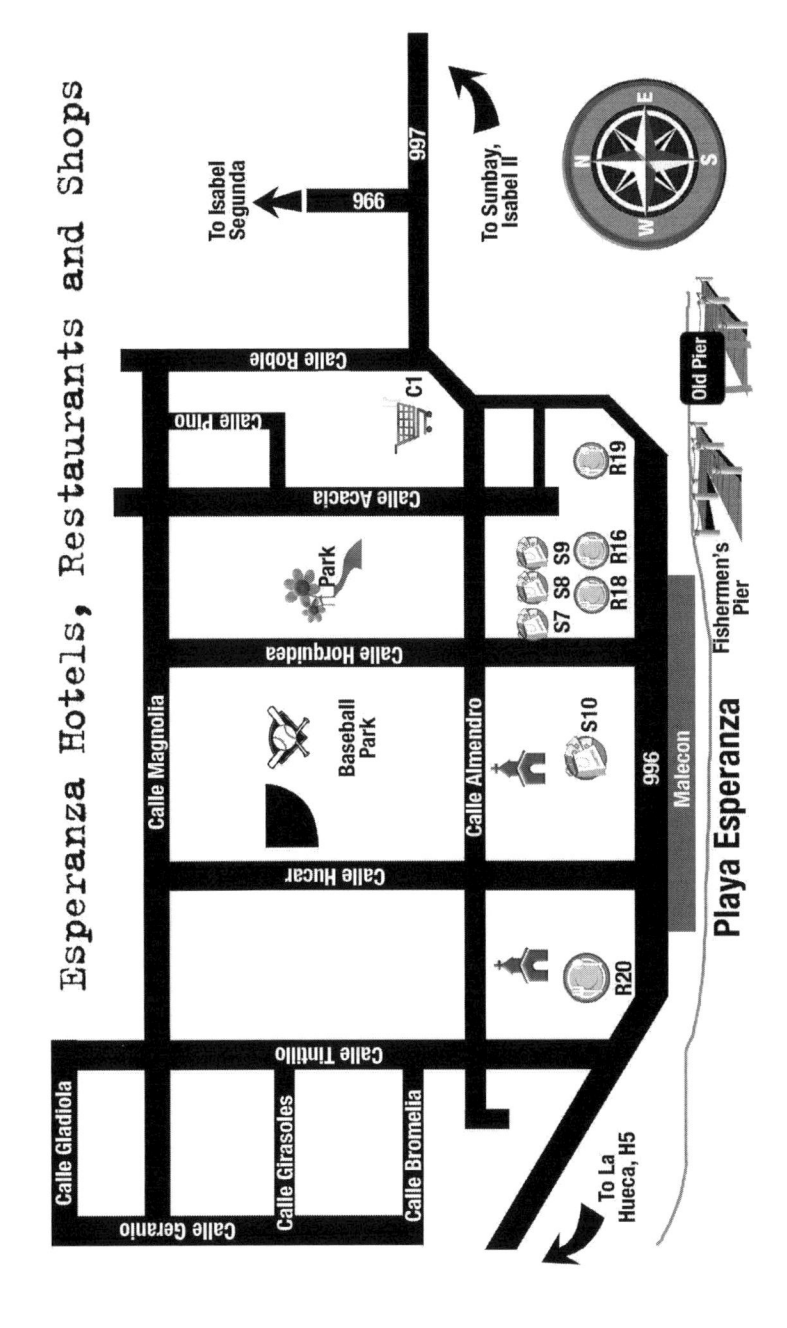

Table Of Contents

Where Now?/Location	25
Why Now?/Why Vieques is Hot, Hot, Hot	29
When Now?/Best Times To Visit	33
What Now?/Island Orientation	37
Get There Now/Two Tickets To Paradise	41
Here Now And Then/A Brief History	47
Swim Here Now/Blissful Beaches	53
Sleep Here Now/Lodging Options	63
Eat Here Now/Island Restaurants	75
Drink Here Now/ Wet Your Whistle	89
Shop Here Now/Treasure Hunting	95
Play Here Now/Active Pursuits	105
Go Wild Here Now/ Flora and Fauna	111
More Here Now/Other Attactions	117
Know Here Now/Practicalities	121

WHERE NOW?

Where Now?

The islands that comprise the upper boundary of the Caribbean Sea are the big ones - Cuba, Jamaica, the Dominican Republic and Puerto Rico. East of Puerto Rico, confident that their larger cousins are doing their job of guarding the warm blue waters of the Caribbean from the gray Atlantic, the islands get significantly smaller and tumble in a relaxed arc southward toward South America. The first of these small gems and the southernmost point of the Bermuda triangle is Vieques, 21 miles long, five miles wide, and leagues apart from its bigger island sister located seven miles to the west.

WHY NOW?

Why Now?

Making a trip to Vieques is a worthwhile endeavor as much for what is there (tempting empty beaches, great restaurants, friendly people) as what is not there -- namely, the US Navy. When the boys in blue pulled up anchor and left Vieques in 2003, after having used the island for target practice for over 60 years, what trailed behind them was a wake of bad feelings. However, they also left behind something far more positive and increasingly rare in the Caribbean – acres and acres of undeveloped Caribbean real estate. This lush green land has since been turned over to the US Fish and Wildlife Service and is now officially the largest and most biologically-diverse national wildlife refuge in the entire Caribbean. And, while a sizeable portion of the land is still off-limits to tourists due to ongoing clean-up efforts, there are still enough perfectly safe, practically deserted, and patently dazzling beaches backed by nothing but palm trees, mesquite bushes, and almond trees to entrance any visitor for days on end.

WHEN NOW?

When Now?

The weather on Vieques is particularly bliss-inducing from mid-November through the beginning of June. Days tend to be dry and breezy with temps in the 80 to 85 range with nights sometimes cooling down to the low 70s. Accordingly, that's when prices at the island's hotels are at their highest. June through November, prices tend to drop dramatically, while temperatures and humidity climb only slightly (85 -90 during the day, 75-80 at night.) September and October have been known to be oppressive with buckets of rain, high heat, high humidity and very few breezes. However, this being a small island, and with weather around the globe leaving everyone guessing, each season brings new surprises.

WHAT NOW?

What Now?

While Vieques is 21 miles long, only approximately 5 miles of this land is developed and inhabited. In that area, the action (such as it is) breaks down pretty much between the island's only two towns: **Isabel Segunda** on the North shore and **Esperanza** on the south shore. On the island's eastern and western boundaries you'll find former navy-occupied lands that are now protected wildlife refuges harboring gorgeous beaches.

Population: 9,000

Isabel Segunda. By day, Isabel Segunda (which you may see written as Isabel II, named after the unpopular Queen of Spain who ruled from 1843-1868) is often hot, dusty, crowded and not the most charming spot Vieques offers its visitors. It is, however, home to the only bank, post office, cash machines, and pharmacies on the island, so a trip to town might be unavoidable. By night, several of the fine dining establishments on the island and three of its best bars are in full swing. But don't worry – come dinnertime, the temperature has cooled down and the streets have less cars and more locals riding down the street on horseback.

Esperanza. Even though it may sound like a villain from the latest superhero movie, "Malecon" actually means promenade. And it is the Malecon that defines the little village of Esperanza. On one side of this balustrade-bedecked walkway sparkles the Caribbean, complete with a modest assembly of bobbing boats and the green-clad uninhabited island of Cayo Afuera (good snorkeling can be had around this island's western side – it's a long swim or quick kayak). On the other side of the Malecon, a colorful collection of bars, shops and characters fit what most people think of when they think quintessential Caribbean. This is a great town to grab a bite to eat, wash it down with a Medalla (the local beer) and join in the activity – which mostly consists of feeding a scrap or two to one of the mellow local dogs; nodding to a few of the old men sitting on the benches under the almond and sea grape trees; and mingling with other tourists, local "gringos" and Viequenses ... as time goes by, island style.

GET HERE NOW

Get Here Now

Most journeys to Vieques require a trip through the San Juan airport. From there several small airlines operate daily flights (on equally small planes) to Vieques. Flights take about 25 minutes and cost, on average, $90 each way. A secondary option is to take an hour or so taxi ride from the airport to the eastern town of Fajardo and from there board a ferry for the approximately hour-and-a-half crossing to Vieques. The taxi costs roughly $75 each way, but the ferry is a bargain at $2.00 per person.

Once on Vieques, it is possible to take a *publico*, or van, from the ferry dock or airport to your hotel but most guests go straight to any of the five or so car rental companies to pick up their car. In fact, if you want to see the majority of the island's beaches and sample its various restaurants, <u>a car rental is essential</u> as publicos are not reliable for tourism transport around the island. Daily rental rates range from approximately $60-85.

Airlines

Cape Air – 1-800-3582-0714
Vieques Air Link – 787-741-8331
Air Sunshine – 787-741-7900

Ferry Information

http://www.enchanted-isle.com/vieques/ferry.htm

Sidetrip to El Yunque

A potential benefit of deciding to set out for Vieques from Fajardo instead of flying directly from San Juan, is that it might be possible to pay a visit to El Junque, the rainforest on the main island. El Yunque is located about equidistant between San Juan and Fajardo, so if your flight and/or ferry times line up, you can take a tour of the rainforest and still be in Fajardo in time to catch your chosen means of transport.

It is important to note, however, that this can only be done through the use of guided transport. You can not rent a car in San Juan, drive to Fajardo and take your car on the ferry to Vieques. If you were to rent a car, you would have to leave it in the lot at Fajardo until you returned. Car reservations on the ferries must be made months in advance and sometimes, even with a reservation, you might not get on.

It is best to use a transport service from San Juan that will allow a stop off in the rainforest such as …

Adventure Tours
http://www.adventourspr.com/transfers.html
(787) 530-8311

Julian's Transportation Services
http://islavieques.com/julianstransportationservices.html
(787) 887-5957

Of course, to truly experience the rainforest, a night or two in that area is highly recommended. At **Robin Phillips' Rainforest Cabin** you'll get a rustic room and an outstanding full-day tour with Robin. Actually, it's something of a "tasting tour" of the jungle as he lets you know about – and sample – the edible plants along the way. Another popular rainforest lodging option is **Casa Flamboyant** that has a small pool and easy access to trails, some of which lead to the river and its accompanying waterfalls.

Robin Phillips' Rainforest Cabin
(787) 414-9596
www.elyunquehotels.com/5.html

Casa Flamboyant
www.rainforestsafari.com/flamboy.html
(787) 874-6074

Main Island Lodging

If you need to overnight in San Juan before catching a flight to Vieques the next morning, the airport **Best Western** makes a perfectly acceptable choice if you don't have much time. It is clean and very convenient.

Best Western
www.bestwestern.com/pr/sanjuanairporthotel
Luis Munoz Marin Int'l Airport, San Juan, Puerto Rico, 00937
Phone: 787-791-1700
Fax: 787-791-1248

$220 / April (handwritten)

If you have a bit of time to explore and you want to visit the Old San Juan area, **Hotel El Convento** is a top-of-the-line choice and a member of the prestigious *Small Luxury Hotels of the World* group. A more affordable option in OSJ is the surprisingly stylish **Sheraton** where bargains can often be found through one of the major online hotel booking companies – especially Priceline.com.

Hotel El Convento
www.elconvento.com
100 Cristo Street, Old San Juan, Puerto Rico 00901
Telephone: 787-723-9020
Toll Free: 800-468-2779
Fax: 787-721-2877

Old San Juan Sheraton
www.sheratonoldsanjuan.com
100 Brumbaugh Street, San Juan, Puerto Rico 00901
Phone (787) 721-5100
Fax (787) 721-1111

If you'd prefer to visit San Juan's beach areas, the **InterContinental** in *Carolina* or the **Marriott Courtyard** are good beachfront options in the mid- to upper-price ranges. The **Holiday Inn Express** is an excellent bargain and is just about two blocks from the beach. For a charming non-chain option, check out **Numero Uno Guesthouse**.

InterContinental San Juan Resort & Casino
www.intercontinental.com
Phone (787) 791-6100

Courtyard Isla Verde Beach Resort
http://www.sjcourtyard.com
Phone: (787) 791-0404

Holiday Inn Express
www.hiexpress.com
Phone: (787) 724-4160

Numero Uno Guesthouse
www.numero1guesthouse.com
Phone: (866) 726-5010

For overnighting in Fajardo, the **Fajardo Inn** is well-located, clean and affordable. A much costlier and very impressive resort option would be the **El Conquistador**.

Fajardo Inn
www.fajardoinn.com
Phone: (888) 860-6006

El Conquistador Resort
www.elconresort.com
866-317-8932

HERE NOW AND THEN

Here Now And Then
A Brief History

With palm trees swaying in the tropical breeze, pristine beaches cascading to aquamarine waters, and wild horses grazing lazily in the shade, it's hard to imagine that Vieques (which derives its name from "bieques," the Taino Indian word for small island) has not always been a place of peace and tranquility. In fact, much the opposite is true.

The problems on Vieques began, like on so many other islands in the Caribbean, with the arrival of European colonizers in 1493. That's the year conquistadors from Spain first set foot on Vieques and took to subduing the Taino Indians, the native population. Despite brave fighting on behalf of the Indians, they were conquered and most were moved off of Vieques to become slaves on the main island.

For the next 300 years, despite sporadic and unsuccessful attempts by British, French and Danish explorers to take over the island, Vieques remained largely forgotten – except by pirates who found the island's relative obscurity particularly suited to their lifestyle.

In the early 1800's, colonization of Vieques by the Spanish began in earnest when Frenchman J.J. Maria Le Guillou arrived and served his appointment as the political and military governor of the Spanish Colony of Vieques from 1832 to 1843. (Guillou is often referred to as the "founder" of Vieques, although archeological digs that uncovered the oldest human remains to be found in the Caribbean show that at least someone else "found" Vieques over 4,000 years ago!)

The Sugar Industry

One of Le Guillou's major actions while on Vieques was to develop large coffee plantations which were eventually converted to sugar plantations. The five major sugar plantations, or *centrales*, thrived and, in a way, live on today as the names of several of Vieques's barrios -- Playa Grande, Santa Maria, Puerto Real, Esperanza. During the early part of the 1800's, the labor for these operations came in the form of slaves from various Caribbean locales.

Upon the abolition of slavery in Puerto Rico in 1873, plantation owners turned to the local population for a workforce. These *agregados*, as they were known, were paid only fifty cents a day, locking them into abject poverty. Yet they *were* allowed to maintain their own plot of land on the plantation where they were able to grow a variety of fruits and vegetables, raise a modest amount of livestock, and have access to fertile coastal fishing areas.

In addition to the *agregados*, the plantation owners also employed thousands of black immigrants who arrived on Vieques from Nevis, St. Thomas, St. Kitts, St. Croix and other islands around the Caribbean. These workers were called *jornaleros* and their arrival on Vieques has contributed to its rich present-day cultural and ethnic makeup.

Still, the conditions under the centrales were deplorable and rebellions and strikes grew as the 18th century progressed.

Hope arrived when the United States was ceded Puerto Rico, Vieques and Culebra by Spain as a result of the Spanish American war. This hope was short-lived, however, as it became clear that the United States had very little interest in getting embroiled in the problems of its new Caribbean charge.

As conditions on the plantations continued to deteriorate – a phenomenon that coincided with the decline of the sugar industry as a whole on Vieques – many islanders struck out to seek better lives in St. Croix, St. Thomas, the main island of Puerto Rico, or at the newly-formed navy base on the neighboring island of Culebra.

The Arrival of the Navy

Mention Vieques to many people today, and their response is likely to be, "isn't that the place the Navy is bombing?"

While it is certainly no longer true, the fact that so many people associate the Navy's "exercises" with Vieques is a testament to how agitating the military's presence here truly was.

The Navy first arrived on Vieques in 1941 and began immediately "expropriating" much of the land that was used for farming and sugar cane production. Families were literally thrown off their land, being told to dismantle their homes and pack their livestock and belongings sometimes with only 24 hours notice. These people were moved into the center of the island, the same part of Vieques that is currently inhabited by its 9,000 residents.

In the initial years of the Navy's presence, work was plentiful as a result of the construction of the base and the pier, or *rompeolas*. Within three years however, this work was completed and most Viequenses found themselves out of work – with no construction or sugar cane jobs remaining. Even fishing was interrupted as a result of the propellers from the navy vessels cutting the lines of the traps or *nasas* that the local fishermen used. In 1978, the fishermen were told that they wouldn't be able to go out on the water because NATO would be running exercises around the island for 28 days. When a group of fisherman went to the main island to complain to Naval officers. the solution they received was to "get welfare."

Needless to say, this callous attitude of the government toward the citizens of Vieques caused a great deal of tension on the island. This tension reached a crescendo in 1999 when a bomb was dropped off-course and killed David Sanes, a Viequense security guard.

This event galvanized a protest movement that had been growing since the 1960's and gathered to it many well-known figures from the political arena and entertainment industry such as Ricky Martin, Hillary Clinton, Edward James Olmos, and Jesse Jackson. *Ni una bomba mas*, or "not one more bomb" became the rallying cry of this movement as first spoken by a man nicknamed Tito Kayak – who became the defacto leader of the protests.

Eventually, the protesters were victorious. On June 14, 2001 President George W. Bush announced that military maneuvers would cease on Vieques beginning May 1, 2003.

The Island Today

Where once the sound of bombs could be heard now is the sound of palm fronds clacking and the Caribbean lapping at Vieques's seductive shoreline. Beaches such as Red and Blue which were once the sites of Naval exercises are now the sites of deep relaxation for visitors and residents of the island.

The lands formerly held by the Navy have been turned over the US Fish & Wildlife Service who are undertaking a clean-up effort to restore Vieques to the pristine island it once was. Through the often unfortunate history of Vieques, a silver lining – though small compared to the trials its residents have been put through – can be found in that these lands now comprise the largest Wildlife Preserve in all of the Caribbean.

All areas of the island that are currently accessible by visitors are completely safe and as more become clearede of military debris, it is hoped that they too will open to the public.

The history of Vieques is one filled with turmoil and turbulence. Perhaps now, as the island and its people head into a new millennium, it can begin writing another chapter in its history book – that of peace and prosperity. As a testament to Vieques' emergence from its troubled times, it was voted Best Caribbean Island in a 2008 survey of *Travel and Leisure* magazine readers.

SWIM HERE NOW

Swim Here Now
The Beaches Of Vieques

Without doubt, the best attractions Vieques has to offer visitors are its beaches. All of the typical superlatives used to describe Caribbean beaches apply here – sugary, powdery, turquoise, jade, crystal-clear, baby-blue, palm-fringed. But there are two additional words that apply to Vieques beaches that are not usually found in the lexicon describing idyllic stretches of island sand – *practically deserted*.

Note: Beaches are indicated on main map unless directions are provided.

Sun Bay Beaches

Sun Bay. The entrance to Sun Bay can be found on Rte. 997 on the island's south shore. There is a small gatehouse that charges a $2.00 admission fee – if there happens to be someone sitting at the guard booth. Once inside, your ticket entitles you to all-day multiple-entry access to three gorgeous beaches. The first, **Sun Bay** itself, is a mile-long, crescent-shaped dream of a beach. The sand is golden, the water is glittering, and there are palm-trees aplenty for catching some zzzzzz's in the shade. It is also the favorite beach for the island's horse population which you can find enjoying the various shady spots on the large grassy area that backs the beach. Sun Bay is the only beach with facilities which include showers, toilets and a small eatery that serves good, cheap burritos.

***Hint**: Walk all the way to the western edge of Sun Bay and a little spit of land will take you out to the semi-detached island of Cayo de Tierra. Wearing sandals is advised (even though you might have to wade a bit to get there) because the Cayo is comprised of rough volcanic rocks. If you are energetic, you can scramble up to the top of the small islet for a great view back to Esperanza and Sun Bay.*

Media Luna. Heading east of Sun Bay, the bumpy dirt road leads next to **Media Luna**. This beach is a small delight, at the end of a large protected cove that makes for very calm waters – a favorite spot for families with younger children.

The water is always a particularly beguiling shade of baby blue and the sand slopes very gradually, letting you walk quite a distance out before the water gets deep. The beach itself is narrow, however there are plenty of shaded palm groves and huts where you can dig in for hours of serious daydreaming.

Navio. You could think of Navio as the bad boy beach of Vieques – rugged and wild with a completely irresistible personality. The wind certainly can't keep itself away, blowing waves like kisses toward the sugary-sand shore all day long. This makes it a cool spot for body surfing. Or, if you're not feeling very energetic, you can simply drowse while listening to the sound of the wind in the sea grapes and palm trees that intimately back the beach. Black volcanic outcroppings at either end of Navio hold within their craggy walls several sea caves worth exploring – especially when the surf is calm. Sometimes after storms, Navio's beach disappears for awhile, but this only adds to its elusive allure.

Hint: *Walk to the east end of the beach, find the small path that leads you up and out on the bluff. Keep walking over the rocky terrain and you'll find one of the island's only blowholes.*

Camp Garcia Beaches

The eastern end of Vieques is the site of the former Camp Garcia, the largest section of the land formerly held by the Navy. Because this land has been turned over to the Fish and Wildlife Service, it is now home to one of the most impressive collection of dazzling and often deserted beaches in the Caribbean. Beaches below are listed with both their island name and "navy" name. It is important to note that the beaches in Camp Garcia are only open from 6:00 AM until sunset at which time the main gate is closed. All directions are from the main gate.

Red Beach/Playa Caracas. A graceful semi-circle of white sand welcomes calm waters on one side and visitors – who can take advantage of a small collection of wooden gazebos – on the other. Low, green-capped volcanic bluffs on the western edge provide a darkly dramatic contrast to the electric blue water that laps at its base. A small island, or *cayo* about 100 yards offers an interesting snorkeling opportunity. A popular spot with local families on the weekends. *Approximately 1 ½ miles, make right at blue "Bienvenidos" sign, drive straight to beach.*

Garcia Beach/Playuela. Traveling the road to Red Beach, there is a turnoff to the right leading to Playuela or Garcia Beach. The road gets a bit rough here, but the reward for persevering is a blustery, beautiful beach hidden by thick jungle. Make your way through the short path through the sea grapes and you'll emerge on a living postcard of a beach – frothy white waves dancing on porcelain blue water in the foreground, small green-capped island plunked directly offshore that offers the chance for some decent snorkeling if the surf is calm enough. The limestone cliffs on either end lend the spot a cozy, "no one knows I'm here" feeling. No shade here so be sure to slather on the sunscreen or bring along a beach umbrella. *Follow directions to Red Beach but make second right after turning at sign.*

Secret Beach/Pata Prieta. OK, so maybe it's not all that much of a secret, but it's a good place to have a secretive afternoon with a favorite book, a favorite iPod mix or a favorite friend because it tends to be relatively unoccupied.

To reach Secret Beach, you walk down a small hill which gives it the feel of a private grotto even though it is quite a large sweep of white sand beach. The craggy rock cliffs that bookend the water here keeps the surf calm and the snorkeling good. To see what's swishing around under the sea, head out along either end of the beach; where the water gets a tad more moody, the viewing gets groovy. Not much shade here, so bring an umbrella if you don't want to broil. *Approximately 2 ½ miles make a right at blue trash barrels, take first right and park in lot. If you go over the metal bridge, you've gone too far.*

Blue Beach/Bahia Los Chivos. While it's true that the Navy was less-than-creative in the color-code naming scheme of the various beaches on the island, in this case, they got it right. The water at Blue Beach is truly just that – a variety of jewel-like blues that range from almost diamond clear to a deep, dark lapiz out toward the offshore island. The sand is powdery white and stretches along the shore in a "W" pattern. The western half of the "W" offers a collection of private pull-offs for your car and plenty of space to claim your own section of sun-soaked beach while the eastern half offers several wooden gazebos to provide a bit of shade. For good snorkeling, stand where these two curves meet (the center of the "W") and swim straight out toward the right side of the island. *Approximately 3 miles, after crossing over metal bridge, look for parking nooks on the right.*

Hint: If you drive just past all the pull-offs for Blue Beach and turn right, you'll find yourself driving along a spit of land that juts straight into the sea. Drive until you can't any more and park, then follow the path in front of you. You'll emerge at a windy, wild place that offers great views out to sea and even better back toward the island itself. To the left is a coral strewn beach – fun to explore but remember to take only memories!

Silver Beach/Playa Plata. Although the dirt road that leads through Camp Garcia can get a bit trying, if you head all the way to Silver Beach – the westernmost beach currently accessible to the public – you will be rewarded by an idyllic spot to wash off the road dust. Plus, because of its location, this crescent of pure white sand tends not to get very crowded – except underwater that is, where you'll be able to do some fine offshore snorkeling by hopping in the sapphire water and swimming along either boundary of the cove. *Follow directions to Blue Beach but don't park. Instead, keep driving and take first left then all lefts after that until you arrive.*

Other Beaches

Black Sand Beach. Before you get too excited, this beach only has *some* black sand on it. And it's pretty hard to get to. That being said, if you're in the mood for a little hiking ala the movie *The Beach*, this spot is worth a visit because its setting is just as gorgeous as the rest of the beaches here and chances are good that you'll have it all to yourself. Of course you'll also see some black sand too because when Vieques gets a lot of rain, it washes down the same arroyo (dry river bed) that you'll walk in to find the beach. This rain carries with it tiny portions of black iron magnetite from the island's one volcanic peak, Monte Pirata. The magnetite washes out on the beach where Mother Nature pushes it to the eastern end which, coincidentally, is where you emerge from your hike. Bring along a magnet and see what happens!

To reach it, head west out of Esperanza on Route 996 until you come to a T intersection. Make a left and look for a guardrail and large billboard on the left. Park here and look for the trail that leads behind the guardrail and down the hill through the dry riverbed known as Quebrada Urbana. Although overgrown in spots, persevere along this trail and you'll eventually emerge at the beach.

Gringo Beach. If you've just landed on Vieques and have the irresistible urge to rip off your clothes and get in the water to wash off all of those airplane germs, there's no better place to do it than this roadside beach. Located about one mile east of the airport, Gringo Beach is a great emergency swimming spot; you can pull into the dirt parking lot, walk down a short embankment and be swimming in softly surfy water all in under a minute. Sometimes, just driving past it is enough to infuse you with a tropical baptism of sorts and remind you of what a truly divine island you're visiting. At the end of the small parking lot, is an outcropping where one car can park at a time. If you're lucky enough to be that vehicle, you can watch great sunsets while "parking" with a special someone. A great spot to stargaze while listening to the music of the waves at night.

Playa Esperanza. It's not really so much a beach as it is a glitteringly beautiful stretch of waterfront that laps at the base of the Esperanza's enticing malecon, or boardwalk. That being said, you can still find a few stretches of sand that'll do for a quick dip. People will say that Cayo Afuera, the uninhabited offshore island, is good for snorkeling but it's truly best enjoyed sitting on the steps across from Banana's restaurant with a cold one contemplating the life lived by the owners of the various boats docked between you and it. Still, if you have the urge to peek underwater, be sure to head out to the right side of the island (western) where there is a decent variety of fish and some coral and sea fans growing off the sides of the submerged boulders. A path at the eastern end of Playa Esperanza will eventually lead you to the much more loungeable Sun Bay.

Playa Grande. This is an aptly named beach as it is indeed a grand, sweeping, cinematic treat of a beach. It's usually completely deserted which means you have nothing but its pristine royal palm-fringed, surf-splashed length in your sights as you stroll along looking for bits of sea glass. And walking is really what this beach is designed for. For the most part, the areas where sea meets shore tend to be rocky. But if you stroll along far enough, you'll eventually find sandy-bottomed areas where you can dip in. Walk really far and you'll come upon a few completely private coves formed by the volcanic rock that are ideal for getting as intimate with the sun rays as you desire. Just bring the sunscreen!

Mosquito Pier/El Rompeolas. On the northwestern side of Vieques, Mosquito Pier is a mile long slab of concrete reaching towards the main island of Puerto Rico. In fact, its original purpose was to connect the two islands during World War II. However the tide of the war turned and construction on the pier was halted at its present length. These days it is used for strictly peaceful pursuits such as fishing and swimming, and may soon be the new dock for the inter-island ferry. The beaches that run to either side of the pier are narrow and not the most attractive in Vieques, so the real attraction here is the chance to snorkel along the pier's western (left if you're looking out to sea) side. Rompeolas literally means "break waves" and you'll see why this is appropriate as you glance to the east and see choppy surf, then turn to the west and take in the calm sea – perfect for your underwater exploration of the large rocks used in the construction of the pier that are now dotted with coral and visited by many species of fish. It is an underwater haunt particularly popular with starfish.

Green Beach/Playa Punta Arenas. Part of the former Navy lands on the western side of the island, Green Beach might be better named "Green Strip of Sand" as the actual beach here is quite narrow. That's not to say it isn't worth a visit. The drive itself is pretty, full of marshes and enormous royal palms swaying the in the breeze, and the network of dirt paths that get you around the shoreline have a real Gilligan's Island feel to them. When you enter the Green Beach area, drive all the way to the right and park in one of nooks to explore a good walking beach that offers a truly inspiring view of the main island of Puerto Rico. Walk all the way to the west and you'll come to a point that is usually buffeted by wind and surf and somehow makes it feel like you are on Vieques as it was thousands of years ago. To snorkel, drive all the way to the left when you enter the area and park just before the chain link fence. Walk along the fence to the shore. You are not allowed to go beyond the fence line on the beach. However, if you get in the water (carefully, there are quite a few urchins in the rocky approach), and swim to the left, you'll come upon a decent reef about 25 yards out.

Playa Cofi/Sea Glass Beach. The beach takes some poking around to find, but that keeps it typically deserted. It is located about one-half mile west of Isabel Segunda on the island's north shore. The best way to find it is heading from the airport, drive until you see the Esso Gas Station on your left – about five-to-ten minutes. After the gas station, you'll go over a mini-bridge after which point you should make an immediate left. Follow your innate Aquaman (or woman) senses and head to the coast. The beach is reached by wandering down a small path carved into the side of the bluff. Once you're finally on the beach, the views to Isabel Segunda to the east and the north shore of Vieques to the west should make you feel your efforts were worthwhile. If you need more justification, remember that this beach was named after a pirate – fitting because you can gather up your own booty by scanning the shore for well-polished sea glass. Ahoy!

SLEEP HERE NOW

Sleep Here Now
Lodging Choices

Until the W hotel opens in April, lodging choices on Vieques remain unique, independent ventures filled with as much color and charm as their owners and managers. Most have less than fifteen rooms and each of the properties listed here offers something special.

Ababor Suites. In addition to being well-stocked, clean and charming, these pretty apartments have two other bonuses: one is that they are located about 100 yards to the beach, the other that they include free kayak usage. Being on the north side of the island, the beach isn't one Vieques' best (those tend to be on the south side), but it is still a nice way to start the morning and calm conditions make it good for kids. Two concrete buildings are well-spaced on large grounds, each containing two suites with various bedding arrangements. All suites have private balconies and small kitchens. Additional amenities include satellite TV with DVD player, phone, stereo, books and games, beach gear, and aircon in the bedrooms,. Each of the two buildings also has its own gazebo for outdoor dining and gathering. *Rates range from $120-$170 and discounts are available for weekly stays or for taking an entire building (two suites).* **H1**
www.ababorsuites.com/
ababor@ababorsuites.com
787.435.2841

Abreeze Guesthouse. This is one of the best-loved lodging choices on Vieques by people who've been coming to the island for years. It consists of only two apartments – a one bedroom with two queen-sized beds and a studio – and they are usually booked well in advance by returning guests. Still, if you're looking for apartment-style accommodation with gracious hosts, a pretty pool, and great views it couldn't hurt to give Juergen and Manfred a call. They also have a small selection of vehicles for rent. *$850-$1350 per week.* **H2**
www.vieques-island.com/rentals/abreeze/
abreezevieques@aol.com
787.741.1856

Atlantico. Getting to these rooms that perch above Roy's Coffee Lounge is a bit like falling *up* the rabbit hole – in this case via a very narrow circular staircase that winds its way up the back of the building. The reward for persevering through to the top of the climb is a charming sanctuary of a room that's a bit of a surprise amid the hustle and bustle of Isabel Segunda. The top floor of Roy's holds a large one-bedroom suite complete with grand columns and grander furniture including two comfy queen-sized beds. There is a full kitchen, washer/dryer, luxurious sofa, and a balcony with peeks of the distant ocean. Best of all, there is a private outdoor shower that lets you stand completely naked on a rooftop in the middle of town without anyone being the wiser. Beneath this grand suite are two additional studios that are equally comfy and feature queen beds and balconies. All rooms have A/C. *Third floor suite: $850/week or $200 per night. Studios: $300 per week.* **R10**
http://home.bellsouth.net/p/s/community.dll?ep=87&subpageid=231037&ck
1.800.853.2625

Bananas Guesthouse and Tradewinds. Best-known for their popular restaurants, both of these locations feature simple rooms out back and situate you in a great spot for the action on the Malecon and for walking to Sun Bay. Banana's offers refrigerators in all rooms, free coffee in the morning and a chance to get away from the distractions of TV and phones. *Rates here range from $65 - $80.* Tradewinds also provides guests in-room refrigerators as well as signing privileges at their restaurant, bar and giftshop. *Rates here are $70 for single occupancy and $80 for double. See "Eat Here Now" for map listings.*
www.bananasguesthouse.com
bananasvieques@gmail.com
787.741.8700

www.enchanted-isle.com/tradewinds
tradewns@coqui.net
787.741.8666

Bravo Beach Hotel. Sleek and modern yet simultaneously warm and welcoming, this boutique hotel is located directly

on the ocean on the island's north shore. The property consists of 8 units, one two-bedroom villa, and two pools. The décor is decidedly South Beach chic with rooms featuring A/C, flat screen TVs, iPod docks, Playstations and platform beds. By day, the poolside bar offers guests the chance to mingle with each other while enjoying self-serve cocktails on the honor system. At night, the bar becomes The Palms and welcomes outside visitors – especially local expats who love the setting and friendly bartenders. A creative mix of music along with the lapping surf provide the perfect soundtrack for a stay here. *$190-$550 for villa.* **H4**
http://www.bravobeachhotel.com/
info@bravobeachhotel.com
787.741.1128

Casa Alta Vista. Convenience, comfort, and caring. That's not the official motto of this 11-room guesthouse, but it might as well be. It's conveniently located within walking distance of the Esperanza strip and has a small store downstairs that carries pretty much anything you could need for your Vieques beach break. The rooms are very comfortable and, although basic, many provide great views over the Caribbean and several feature kitchenettes. But perhaps what truly sets this place apart is the caring of owner Mark Biron who will truly go out of his way to make your stay all you need it to be – including outfitting you with one of his scooter or car rentals. Start your days here by picking up some beach gear (modest fee), muffins and free coffee at the convenience (there's that word again) store and end it by climbing up to the rooftop deck, where you can sip something fruity, see the sun splash down and watch the stars put on one hell of a second act. All rooms have AC, free WiFi and refrigerators. *$75 - $95. $175 two-bedroom apartment that sleeps 6.* **H5**
www.casaaltavista.net/
casaaltavista@yahoo.com
787.741.3296

Casa De Amistad. Conveniently located on a side street in Isabel Segunda, just steps from the ferry dock, this laid-back hotel oozes charm. The care of the owners and managers is evident everywhere you look, from the eclectic assembly of antique and island-inspired furniture and artwork, to the

well-stocked communal kitchen, to the open, breezy décor in the rooms, to the charming courtyard featuring a small but very inviting pool. Coffee is served every morning in the kitchen where you are also invited to prepare light meals throughout the day. A small bar room provides a guest computer or you are welcome to connect your own laptop to the complimentary wifi. A communal TV room offers a fun gathering spot but with the various patios and balconies, you might never use it. All rooms feature AC, private baths, mini-fridges and ceiling fans. *$70 - $90.* **H6**
http://www.casadeamistad.com
viequesamistad@aol.com
787.741.3758

Casa Ladera. This spotlessly-clean, perfectly-maintained collection of rental units located on the north shore of Vieques has won many a fan through the owners' unyielding attention to detail. Each of the modern, two-bedroom units feature AC, satellite TV, DVD and VCR with onsite library, free WiFi, beach chairs, coolers, washers and dryers and fully-stocked kitchens. The kitchens can be put to good use as one of the island's two major grocery stores are only minutes away. Glimpses of the ocean can be had through the tropical foliage and a stroll on nearby Sea Glass Beach (see "Swim Here Now") is a great way to start or end each day – usually you'll have all that sand and surf to yourself. If you're more of a pool person, the large in-ground beauty here won't disappoint. The owners will arrange to pick you up at the airport and even provide you with a rental vehicle to explore more of the island. *$1,000 - $2,000 per week. Shorter stays someties available, call for details.* **H7**
www.casa-ladera.com
jen@casa-ladera.com
917.570.7558

Casa La Lanchita. You can't really sleep closer to the surf on Vieques without getting wet than you can at this guesthouse located east of Isabel Segunda's ferry dock in the neighborhood known as Bravos de Boston. All rooms feature queen-sized beds, satellite TV, beach gear, fully-equipped kitchens and – most strikingly – they all have balconies practically suspended out over the sea. The only thing in the way is the charming swimming pool built into the seawall

between you and the ocean, but who would complain about that? Hosts Doug and Marikay McHoul seem to have knack for making guests feel instantly at home
and can help with island orientations as well as provide you with a car rental. Snorkeling at the reef in front of the hotel can bring pleasant surprises. *$95-$140*. **H8**
www.viequeslalanchita.com
LaLanchita@aol.com
787.741.8449
800.774.4717

Crow's Nest. The Crow's Nest is tucked into the hills between Esperanza and Isabel Segunda. There are 16 rooms to choose from, mostly small and simple but all with the added benefit of a kitchenette. The pool here is situated in the middle of very pretty garden and offers a great spot to soothe that hard-earned sunburn at day's end. The overall feeling here is like renting a room in a large home, with lots of nooks, crannies and staircases to explore around the building. The extensive grounds are also home to the Island Steakhouse Restaurant that hosts a well-attended Tuesday night happy hour from 5-7pm where you have a chance to win your bar tab (see *Eat Here Now*). *$124 - $245*. **H9**
http://www.crowsnestvieques.com/
thenest@coqui.net
1-877- CROWSNEST

Enchanted Garden. This unique lodging establishment on the island's north shore is all about flexibility. And we're not talking about that of the uber-fit spin instructor/owner, Violet -- although her delightful hospitality would be reason enough to stay here. We're talking rooming flexibility. A main house offers a three-bedroom unit on the top floor complete with kitchen and TV room and a two-bedroom apartment on the first. These two units can be combined to provide a six-bedroom (the sitting room can become a bedroom) house rental. A separate building currently houses a small but well-thought-out studio complete with kitchenette plus six newly constructed studios with king-sized beds, small refrigerators, DVD and CD players, AC, WiFi access and outdoor balconies or patios. All units are immaculately clean and thoughtfully outfitted with all you need for vacation success. The charming grounds feature

dozens of species of mango trees, gorgeous frangipani, near constant breezes and delightful landscaping as well an area for spin classes and the popular Coqui Fire Café (see *Eat Here Now*). *Weekly rates range for $500 to $3000 for six-bedroom house and include the seventh night free. Daily rates available upon request.* **H10**
www.enchantedgardeninn.com
violet@enchantedgardeninn.com
787.741.2805

Evamer. Situated on a sloping hillside directly above the beach on the north shore of Vieques, this collection of 4 private villas and two studios has one of the most idyllic settings of any lodging facility on Vieques. Guests can relax by the small but perfectly-situated pool or take the private staircase down to the beach. Every unit has A/C, TV, kitchenette and, perhaps most importantly, a view of the ocean. And, while the grounds and buildings of Evamer certainly make a stay here worthwhile, the real star of the show is the personable manager, Mark, who will pick you up from the airport, help you with rental cars and give you advice that only a local could. *$135 - $250.* **H11**
http://www.evamer.com
reservations@evamer.com
787.741.2303

Hacienda Tamarindo. One of the island's few bed and breakfasts, Hacienda Tamarindo offers guests lodging in one of 16 rooms ranging from standard to multi-room suites to a newly opened private villa. The views from various vantage points around the hotel are glorious – especially from the perfectly situated pool. An old tamarind tree grows straight up through the main lobby where the friendly staff is always at the ready to help you enjoy Vieques and an honor bar offers up drinks and snacks. The hearty and highly-regarded breakfast is served outdoors on an upstairs patio and features daily specials. *$125 - $325.* **H12**
www.haciendatamarindo.com
hactam@aol.com
787.741.0420

Hector's By The Sea. If you've ever dreamed of having your own little love shack (or writer's retreat, or family

hideaway, or party hut, or ... you get the picture) by the sea, you can make that dream a reality by staying at Hector's. This property features three casitas placed in such a way that there is nothing but your own thoughts to get in the way of looking across the grassy field to the sea -- and a few well-timed rum and pineapple cocktails should even take care of those. The casitas all have AC, ceiling fans, refrigerators, microwaves, coffeemakers, private baths, and perfectly-placed hammocks on balconies overlooking the small pool and Jacuzzi. Two casitas have two queen beds, and the other has just one. Beach towels, chairs, and coolers are provided. *$115 - $165.* **H13**
http://www.hectorsbythesea.com/
info@hectorsbythesea.com
787.741.1178

Hix Island House. Hix Island House is certainly not for everyone. However, if you don't mind a little rain getting on your bedroom floor, a few birds (and/or bugs) perching briefly on your kitchen counter, or doing without air conditioning and television during your visit, there simply is no better place on Vieques to experience the natural side of the island. Hix consists of three buildings scattered about its 5 acre jungle setting – one round, one square and one triangular – each holding a variety of "lofts". The buildings and the rooms themselves are architecturally striking and have a Zen-like simplicity. Typically, the front wall of each unit is open air, allowing unfettered access to private patios -- the perfect locales from which to enjoy the sound of the wind in the trees and the coqui frogs singing at night. All lofts feature kitchens stocked with homemade bread and other breakfast items. Most have private, outdoor showers. *$185 - $295.* **H14**
http://www.hixislandhouse.com
info@hixislandhouse.com
787.741.2302

Inn on the Blue Horizon. There are two things that really work for this hotel. The first is evident in the property's name. The Inn on the Blue is located on top of a beautiful bluff that looks out over the glittering Caribbean. The second is the hotel's pool. While it is just a large rectangle, it

too is situated to take in the intoxicating views and be caressed by the near-endless breeze. Rooms, which are decorated in a rich collection of antiques and feature AC, are arranged around the property in individual bungalows each housing two units. Should you decide to stay here, you might want to give the once-great bar and restaurant a pass as the food is inconsistent at best and the staff tends toward a level of apathy that is unusual even in the Caribbean. Tennis courts and weekly activities such as volleyball and live music performances round out the offerings here. **H15** *$125 - $400.*
http://www.innonthebluehorizon.com/
info@innonthebluehorizon.com
877.741.BLUE (2583)

La Finca Caribe. Set in the hills in the middle of the island, this unique property has a relaxed, hippyish vibe. Rooms are found either in the main house which features a communal kitchen, open-air living room and jungle-wrapped deck or in rustic wooden cottages nearby. A stay here is akin to cabin camping – with shared baths and public, outdoor showers – but in a charming, colorful environment. A large pool and assortment of hammocks strategically placed around the three-acre landscape make it easy to relax the day away while listening to nothing but the breezes lazily blowing by. *$65 - $115.* **H16**
www.lafinca.com
manager@lafinca.com
787.741.0495

Seagate Hotel. Perched on a hillside near the fort above Isabel Segunda, this quirky hotel occupies an unlikely but very likeable location. Its warren of rooms is arranged horizontally along a hillside shaded by thick jungle trees. Rooms have kitchenettes and balconies but are otherwise basic. Each, however, is lovingly appointed with unique artwork and thoughtful touches to make the place feel like home. Breakfast, which is included in the reasonable rates, is delivered right to your room. Late check-outs can be arranged for a modest fee of $10.00 and the property offers wireless Internet for $2.00 a day. The owner of Seagate,

Penny, has been instrumental in founding and helping the Vieques Humane Society to thrive. Her love of animals is reflected in the horses she keeps on site which you are welcome to visit with or even ride during your stay. Proceeds from the rides help support the work of the Society. All rooms have fans, some with AC. *$80 - $140.* **H17**
http://www.seagatehotel.com
concierge@seagatehotel.com
787.741.4661

Tropical Guest House. Situated in a typical island neighborhood just on the outskirts of Isabel Segunda, this charming guest house offers a variety of basic but sparkling clean rooms at some of the best prices on Vieques. "Single" rooms feature one double bed, "doubles" hold a double bed and a single, and three studios with private kitchens accommodate four to six people each. All rooms feature AC, TV and private bathrooms. The onsite World Café offers a great spot for breakfast and evening cocktails and conversation with the Guest House's young, warm and knowledgeable owners, Joe and Maria. *$60 -$105.* **H18**
http://www.viequestropicalguesthouse.com/
jb@viequestropicalguesthouse.com
787.741.2449

W Retreat and Spa. The ultra-pampering W hotel chain gets it's name from "whatever, whenever" indicating just how far the staff will go to accommodate the needs of their clientele. For the past several years on Vieques however, locals joked that it really referred to the date by which the Martineau Bay Resort would be morphed into a W property because it always got pushed further and further into the future. It looks like it's really going to happen though, with notices on the hotel's website proclaiming an opening on 30 April 2009. Not sure what we'll find behind the gates, but the former resort had a pretty location, with two smallish beaches in coves. An infinity-edged pool promises to take advantage of the often sunset-splashed view back to the main island. It's bound to be super-chic. And super-expensive. **H19** www.starwoodhotels.com 787.741.4100

Rental Homes

From simple concrete homes in traditional Viequense neighborhoods, to pool-bedecked villas perched on mountainsides with quiver-inducing views, there is quite a range of properties for rent on Vieques. If having the ability to cook your own food and secure a greater degree of privacy than what you'd get in a hotel is important, you might want to check with one of the following realty companies to plan your self-catered stay.

Rainbow Realty
http://www.enchanted-isle.com/rainbow/
787.741.4312

Guayacan Realty
http://www.guayacanrealty.com/
787.741.0414

Connections Real Estate
http://www.enchanted-isle.com/connections/
787.741.0023

Island Real Estate
http://www.islandrealestate.net/
787.741.7001

Vieques Realty and Rentals
http://www.viequesrealtyandrentals.com/
787.741.0330

EAT HERE NOW

Eat Here Now
The Restaurants of Vieques

For a little island, Vieques certainly shows its love for food in the many dining options available. Like most places on the island, restaurants are basically divided between the island's two main towns – Isabel Segunda in the north and Esperanza in the south ...

Local Flavor

The Puerto Rican love of *comida* is evident in the various food outposts scattered around the island. These range from the sturdy food trucks outside of the Sun Bay entrance to small mom-and-pop kiosks on the side of the roads consisting of not much more than a plastic table-and-chair set and a gas grill. While weekends are the most popular time for these operations to set up shop, you should be able to find a bit to bite nearly any day of the week. Here's a quick primer on what you might expect to find at these affordable slices of true local flavor:

Pinchos. Consisting of skewered cubes of marinated and grilled beef, pork or chicken, these tasty tidbits are what you'll find being sold by most of the roadside grills. You can usually get them de-sticked onto some type of white bread and boosted by a bit of hot sauce.

Arepas. These pockets of pleasure are the Puerto Rican version of a biscuit. They are made from corn flour and can be either fried, boiled or baked. While they're great on their own (there are few things better to use to scoop up those last few forkfuls of rice and beans), you can also find arepas stuffed with various meats and spices.

Mofongo. You'll probably find this more at proper restaurants than kiosks, but it's well worth seeking out. Sort of like a shepherd's pie, Mofongo is made of garlicky mashed plantains layered over the top of seasoned beef, chicken or seafood. It's fantastically filling so watch the appy's and desserts when you're adding it to your plate (and your waistline)!

Empanadas and Pastelillos. All cultures have their versions of the dumpling – some type of yummy starch stuffed with some type of yummy filling. In Puerto Rico these dumplings take the form of empanadas and pastelillos, which consist of a flaky pastry-like outer wrappings concealing a mix of meat, veggies and spices inside. They're deep-fried and highly addictive.

Alcapurrias. A popular treat with locals on beach days, alcapurrias consist of ground plantains rolled into balls around a filling of meat or crab and spices. They are deep-fried (seeing a pattern here yet?).

Rice. You'll find the white staple served up two ways on Vieques. *Arroz con habichuelas* is rice and beans – perhaps the most comforting of all comfort foods. And *arroz con gandules* is rice and pigeon peas – small, bean-like nuggets that add an earthy, nutty flavor.

Pastelles. If you happen to be on the island around the holidays and have access to your own kitchen, keep your eyes open for signs advertising pastelles for sale. These treats take hours to make, and are like nicely-wrapped Christmas presents, consisting of seasoned ground beef or chicken often mixed with such flavorants as prunes, raisins, capers, and olives all pressed and packaged in a folded banana leaf. If you are lucky enough to find them, they are usually sold frozen, so all you need to do is drop them in some boiling water for about 30-40 minutes, unfold and go to chow-down town!

Isabel Segunda And Environs

Barefot Be'stro. Located across from Bravo Beach Hotel in Bravos de Boston, this casual eatery feels like a typical island beach bar. Only thing is, it's not on the beach – it's actually at someone's home in the eclectic Bravos De Boston neighborhood. But the picnic tables, fishing nets and overall laid-back vibe almost make you not miss the surf. Besides, the taste of the sea is just a bite away as you enjoy the exceptionally fresh fish dishes. Serves lunch and dinner that include plenty of choices beyond seafood. **R1**
340.514.0124

The Blue Crab. The modernist exposed-concrete décor at this restaurant belies the comforting nature of its menu which features such selections as *Maryland Blue Crab Cakes*, *Mainlanders Ribeye Steak*, and *Double Fudge Cake* for dessert. Stop by for lunch and give one of the paninis a try (or take a few to the beach). Creations include *Pulled Pork and Swiss*, *Flank Steak and Provolone*, *Grilled Chicken with Spinach and Havarti* and *Burger Melts*. **R16**
787.741.1147

BBH. Once a thriving collection of rooms, restaurants and nightlife, the latest news is that the eateries have been closed here due to a change in management. Worth giving a call to see if anything has changed once you are on the island. **R2**
http://www.bravobeachhotel.com/BBH_REST.html
787.741.1128

Coconuts. This collection of little wooden huts is the kind of place you might expect to come upon after first disembarking on any number of tropical islands. And while the ferry dock is a few blocks away from this landlocked joint, it somehow retains the feeling of being surfside. The food is simple, good and affordable and features such straight-up eats as burgers, meatloaf, ribs and fish and chips. The coconut tarts get rave reviews! **R13**
www.coconutsvieques.com   787.741.9325

El Patio. Chef Carlos Alzogaray used to make magic at the former Uva restaurant. At publication time, he has joined Sonia Romero, the owner of this casual little eatery named because of its roadside brick patio, to serve up Latin and Puerto Rican dishes. Whatever this chef touches turns to gold so definitely stop in to check out the culinary alchemy. **R3**   787.741.6381

El Resuelve. If you want to truly dine like the locals, this place can't be beat – especially for their exceptional pastelillos. It's an open-air little joint where you'll sit at plastic table and chair sets and dine on delicious and affordable food. Grab a Medalla and a heaping plate of *arroz con pollo* or *crab empanadas* and you'll feel more and more like a Viequense with each bite. Keep your eye out for the big sign on the left after you've passed the hospital and fire department heading away from Isabel Segunda on Route 997. The restaurant is on the corner.
787.741.1427

Mamasongas. In its simple setting, this restaurant consistently delivers high-quality meals at affordable prices such as cut-with-your-fork *Beef Tenderloin* and *Linguine with Clam Sauce*. Located directly across the street from Al's Mar Azul (see *Drink Here Now*), it's a great spot to watch the action (or inaction) there and also to take in the nightly parade of ferry passengers carrying home their treasures from the main island.
No phone number available. **R4**

Mia's Pizza. Both native Viequenses, the owners of this done-right eatery, Maria and Efrain lived in New York for awhile (Maria has even cooked for Mayor Bloomberg!). While there, they clearly got the knack for making pizza "old school style" as Efrain has been known to boast. In fact, close your eyes and take a bite of the thin crust, superb sauce with just the right amount of oily goodness, and great mozzarella and you might think you're back in Coney Island in its good days. In addition to the perfecto pies the duo also cooks full-on dinners and lunches that get raves in a style that can best be described as Puerto Rican/American/Italian fusion. Pizzas can be delivered so be sure to put this number in your Blackberry before arriving. **R5**
787.741.3789

Mr. Sushi. This is the only spot on Vieques to get sushi so the food quality could slide – but it doesn't. Maybe that's because Mr. Sushi is used to serving discerning customers at his outpost on Long Island where he spends summers. That being said, this spot is only a sushi restaurant for the high season – from approximately November through June. During that time, stop by to get some super-fresh fish and other Japanese creations served up by smiley Mr. Sushi himself along with his delightful wife.   Lunch everyday except Wednesday and Thursday, dinner every night but Wednesday. **R11**   787.741.2828

Oasis Café. The only food outlet directly on the newly remodeled Plaza in Isabel Segunda, this charming gazebo offers you the chance to grab a pastry, cup of coffee, shake, frape, or bowl of soup, take a seat under one of the shady trees and watch the island world go by – sometimes on horseback, often to the beat of reggaeton. **R6**
787.530.2707

Panadaria Viequense. Boy do they do sandwiches right at this locally-owned joint. The creations, ranging from the king of sandwiches – the Cubano – to the humble ham and cheese, to over 20 other variations are all made on the yummy house bread and pressed in a grill to give them that warm, melty, crunchy goodness that might make you order seconds. To eat your sandwich while warm, pull up a plastic chair and grab a table in the simple surroundings or else get it brown-bagged and enjoy under a palm on your favorite beach. You can call in your order ahead of time to preserve those minutes by *el mar*. **R7**
787.741.8213

Peter's. It's truly amazing how much of the world Chef Peter can fit in this small but charming restaurant. There's *Moroccan Hummus*, *Hand-Rolled Gnocchi*, and the drool-inducing *Puerto Rican Pierogies* served with caramelized onions and sour cream. And those are just the starters. Mains continue the transglobal taste fest with creative dishes like *Louisiana Shrimp 'N Grits*, *Mexican Pulled Pork*, *Rasta-House Jerk Chicken* and *Salmon Roasted with Herbes De Provence*. An equally creative approach to day-of-the-week

dining means you should check with Peter's when you're on Vieques to see if you'll be there on Vegetarian, Creole or Burger night. French press coffee, cappuccino and espresso in addition to strong and seductive drinks like coconut and passion fruit martinis keep the rails of this multi-culti meal train well-lubricated. **R8**
www.peters-vieques.com
787.741.0269

Richard's Cafe. This restaurant that specializes in traditional Puerto Rican food such as *mofongo*, *pastelillos*, and *arepas fritas* gives new meaning to the "slow food" movement. The staff is friendly, the pleasant space is clean and nicely air conditioned, and, when the food arrives, it is always tasty. But. Wait. You. Will. Bring along a good book or good company and settle in for the night. Steaks, chicken dishes, soups and seafood are also available. **R9**
787.741.5242

Roy's Coffee Lounge. Vieques has been a bit slow to get with the coffee revolution – perhaps because there are precious few places to get the jolt of caffeine needed to open a coffee shop. You can now get a cup of coffee at several colmados, one of the gas stations, and the bakery. But these tend to be perfunctory affairs, better for the tingle than the taste. Roy's, however, is a proper café with properly-made caffeine creations. Choose from straight-up coffee and espresso or indulge in creative lattes like *Chocolate Raspberry*, *Mocha* and the well-loved *Snickers* featuring chocolate, caramel and almond flavors. Food options include all-day breakfast burritos, beef or chicken tacos and chicken salad wraps. The cool art-filled interior space is made even more so by the cranking air conditioning, while a small courtyard lets you sip your drinks in the outdoors. WiFi connection is available for free, two (usually) soundless flat-screen TVs give you windows to the outside world if you choose to look, and an eclectic soundtrack helps boost the effects of the java. At night during high-season Roy's becomes a fun bar where locals and tourists get buzzed on more than just caffeine. **R10**
787.741.0685

Shauna's. A good spot for lunch, this no-nonsense place offers a selection of traditional Puerto Rican food served up cafeteria style. Just grab a tray, point at the food behind the glass, pay a little bit of money, then sit down, tuck in, and be prepared to get nice and full. Get there on the early side. They close when the grub is gone – and it goes fast! **R12**
787.741.1434

Taverna. You body might be basking in the Caribbean sun, but that doesn't mean your mouth can't wander – culinarily that is. Treat it to a vacation-within-a-vacation with Mediterranean menu items like *Sheeps Milk Ricotta Ravioli in Pesto with Pistachios and Viequense Basil* and *Pollo alla Mattone with Lemon, Rosemary Polenta and Spinach*. Fresh, creative ingredients and perfectly balanced flavors and textures shine in specials like *Sardinian Saffron Dumplings with Hot Sausage and Tomato* as well as *Chickpea Fritters with Goat Cheese and Caponata*. Sophisticated martinis such as *Rosemary Pear* and *Basil Strawberry* along with homemade *Limoncello* get you in the mood for the euro-fest while digestivos like *Fernet Branca*, and *Grapas* settle things down at the end. Gourmet takeout items include *Hummus, Wheatberry Salad, Szechuan Eggplant,* and more. Mama Mia! Open for lunch and dinner. **R13**
787.741.7760

Topacio. At times, the service here is so indifferent as to pretty much be non-existent. However, if you don't mind being ignored for awhile (and you're on vacation, so what else do you have to do?), you can try out some *chicken quesadillas, tostones rellenos* or *stuffed plantains*, or a selection of seafood prepared with local sauces by a local chef. **R14**
787.741.1179

Williams's Pizza. Icy cold AC and steamy hot pizza on the main street in Isabel Segunda makes this a great spot to stop in if you're running errands in town. Small pizzas start at just $8. Or just grab a slice and get to the beach! **R15**
787.741.8396

Catering

Aguacate Catering. The guys that own this moveable feast used to own a restaurant in Provincetown, Rhode Island, so they know a thing or two about provisioning people who are on vacation. If you're renting a house on the island, a good option might be to give them a call in advance to set yourself up with some fine home-cooked food. They'll cater for 2 to 100 people whether it's a quiet dinner, cocktail party or wedding. Their Mediterranean stylings are truly scrumptious.
aguacatecatering@yahoo.com
787.615.2320   787.599.0539

Esperanza

Bananas. An island icon, Bananas has been serving up cold drinks, bar-and-grill style food, and good times for years. The setting is funky, casual, open-air and definitely very Vieques. They are probably most famous for their burgers and homemade potato chips, but you can also enjoy sandwiches, hot dogs, stuffed potatoes, salads, tostones, Caribbean fish cakes, and a small selection of served-all-day dinners including jerk chicken and grilled pork chops or fish. A creative bar menu will truly help you get on island time and an upstairs deck bar that is open during high season provides a relaxed and sometimes hopping venue for locals and visitors to mingle. **R16**
787.741.8100
http://bananasguesthouse.com/menu.htm

Bayaonda Artisan Breads. If you love a good loaf of bread, it's worth checking this baxter's (female baker) website before coming down to Vieques. If you're in luck, it will be one of the weekends when Viequense Chef Wanda Rivera, formerly of Bayaonda restaurant, is baking a variety of artisanal breads which she does every other Saturday. They can be ordered online and picked up at the Vieques Conservation and Historical Trust in Esperanza.
www.bayaonda.com

Bellybuttons. No matter how much or how little you eat at this casual outdoor spot for breakfast and lunch, you might want to contribute a shot of your bellybutton which will be posted somewhere around the joint on one of the wooden beams that hold up the corrugated metal roof. The vibe is friendly and the menu is simple and affordable, featuring a selection of traditional breakfast foods and a solid choice of lunches including great sandwiches and daily specials. If you don't feel like sitting, Craig and Norma can pack up your lunch for you to take to the beach – call ahead to have it ready when you arrive. **R17**
787.741.3336

Duffy's Esperanza. Duffy, a Caribbean legend himself, has opened many a bar/eatery on Vieques. His latest project is actually run by his son Mikey and features the always-

winning formula of a casual environment, friendly bar staff, and good food at reasonable prices. Selections include great burgers, fish tacos, cubano sandwiches and nightly specials that demonstrate the chef's ability to move well beyond bar food. **R18**
787.741.7600

El Quenepo. Open, airy and reminiscent of a breezy Cuban café, El Quenepo sits at the east end of the Esperanza restaurant strip. The well-prepared food here has a whimsical and definitely Caribbean vibe with such dishes as *Pineapple Guava Glazed Pork Ribs*, *Calypso Corn Chicken* and *Chorizo Served Over Fresh Fettuccini*, and the complex and deliciously vegetarian *Rasta pasta*. Nightly specials round out the menu and showcase the kitchen's true skill. The upscale dining here goes great after a grungy night in the biobay! **R19**
787.741.1215

Tradewinds. Get to this longstanding Esperanza icon before the light fades from the day, grab one of the tables by the edge of the porch and you'll be treated to a great dinner surpassed only by the view. Tradewinds indisputably has the best vantage point of any restaurant on Vieques, looking out over the Caribbean Sea toward the tiny, uninhabited island of Cayo Afuero. The menu is equally attractive. Choose from fresh fish prepared in your choice of styles including *Grilled with Pineapple Salsa* or *Corn-Encrusted with Toasted Almond Butter*. Or select from a variety of Caribbean specialties like mofongo, churassco or fresh lobster. Also a great spot to gaze at the sea and share a super-fresh super-sized salad for lunch or start the day with a good-sized breakfast. **R20**
787.741.8666

Elsewhere on the Island

Coqui Fire Café. Patty and Jim Cochran have long been teasing and tingling tastebuds on the island and nationwide with their all-natural Coqui Fire hot sauce. Available in nine varieties like *Pina Colada Mustard* and *Komodo Dragon*, the little bottles of fiery flavor featuring ingredients like vanilla, cumin, ginger root and brandy make great gifts for people back home. While on Vieques though, be sure to reserve a seat (they do sell out – every time), at the Coqui Fire Café, a small open-air affair located on the Enchanted Garden Inn. On Tuesday and Thursday nights from 5-9 they serve up huge, delicious portions of Mexican food at seriously good prices. BYO beer or wine to go with such dishes as *Chicken Mole Enchiladas*, *Chili Rellenos* or the stuffed-full, super-filling *Big Kahuna Burrito*. **R21**
www.coquifire.com
coqui@coquifire.com
787.435.1099

Isla Nena Café. Viequense Eddie Perez and Floridian wife Teresa Lynn have opened this long-closed café at the Vieques Airport. A great spot to grab an early breakfast (they start serving at 5:30 am) or a snack to keep your stomach from getting cranky while you wait for your flight to depart. Selections include omelets, pancakes and breakfast sandwiches in addition to wraps, pressed sandwiches and burgers. **R22**
www.islanenacafe.com
787.741.4111

Island Steakhouse. A better name for this island institution located at the Crow's Nest Hotel might be Island Steak *Tree*house because dinners are served up on a (usually) breezy deck set at palm-frond level. Here they deliver the island's best selection of Angus beef – all served with Ceasar Salad or the ever-popular Island Wedge served with Blue Cheese and bacon bits. In addition to doing steaks well (or rare or medium, of course), the Steakhouse also serves up ribs, surf and turf, seafood and burgers. Come for Happy Hour on Tuesday nights, score a chance to win your bar bill, then settle in for some serious dining. If you've

room left, you can kill off any remaining hunger pangs with a decadent *Death By Chocolate* dessert. **R23**
www.crowsnestvieques.com/islandsteakhouse
787.741.0011

The Shack. The name pretty much says it all about this tin-roofed shanty located in the cooler green interior of Vieques. Formerly and sometimes presently known as *Chez Shack*, it's truly anybody's guess when or if this location will be open. But if you're on the island, it's worth asking because when they're doing their thing it's one of the yummiest most fun spots to grab some food on the island. They occasionally host a reggae grill night where you can eat grilled meats and selections from a salad bar to the accompaniment of a live band that has plenty of salsa in their Jamaican rhythms. **R24**
787.741.2175

DRINK HERE NOW

Drink Here Now

Unlike the reggae beach splashes in Jamaica, the full moon parties on Tortola or the carnival spirit that pervades partying in Trinidad, nightlife on Vieques is fairly tame. For many visitors the only sparkly lights they see at night are in the water at the bio bay. Still, there are just enough watering holes to fill your nights with good drinks, good company and good fun ...

Isabel Segunda

Al's Mar Azul. Quick, remember the last really fun party you went to? The one where you might not necessarily have known everyone but you felt really comfortable talking to anyone? The one where the music was just right, the drinks went down a little too easily and everything just seemed to click? That's what it's like at this quintessential Caribbean bar nearly every night of the year. Helping to create the perpetual-party vibe are a foosball table, dartboard, a kicking soundtrack that changes with the highly-competent bartenders, and an assortment of friendly regulars that add true character to the joint. Then, of course, there's the nightly light show on the outside deck that happens when Mom Nature slam dunks the sun behind the island ridges. Of course, the whole shebang is presided over by Al who, like a benevolent Caribbean God of Good Times seated in his usual post at the bar, will usually be more than happy to accept your offering of a tequila shot. Saturday nights feature karaoke, but it's of the low-key kind and easy to ignore if you're so inclined; but the quality of some of the island voices might just inspire you to grab the mic. But please, no *Summer Nights*. **B1**
marazul@coqui.net
787.741.3400

Bar Plaza. In the center of Isabel Segunda is a euro-style, open-square, newly refurbished plaza. On the south side of this plaza is a bar that hasn't been refurbished -- ever. It is a simple square cement structure with a veteran pool table in the middle and a bar that runs the length of the place along one wall. All the other walls have floor to ceiling openings that make the place feel like it would fit well in an old Clint

Eastwood western. Beers are cheap, the nearly always all-Viequense patrons are friendly, and the juke box in the corner plays a colorful mix of Latin fiesta music that dramatically brighten things up. Grab a Medalla and one of the cement benches out front and let the low-key bustle of town cruise by. And when you go back inside for your second round, obey the sign above the bar and *cuide su vocabulario*. This is a respectable joint, after all. **B2**
787.741.2176

The Palms at BBH. This small bar offers big fun. It's located in the BBH complex (see *Sleep Here Now*) adjacent to a very cool pool that gets more alluring as the drinks go down. In keeping with the BBH vibe, the setting is chic although the friendly regulars keep things down to earth. Still, bathed in the atmospheric lighting and inventive soundtrack you can't help but feel a little exta-fabulous. **R2**
www.bravobeachotel.com
787.741.0490

Sombrero Viejo. According to its ad in the monthly "what's on" magazine, Vieques Events, this watering hole, smack dab in the center of Isabel Segunda is "OPEN EVERYDAY FROM SOMETIME AT ABOUT MIDDAY TO SOMETIME AT ABOUT MIDNIGHT." It is just this type of smarmy attitude that prevails at Kuhn's, the last name of the bar's owner and the name by which most locals call the bar. Kuhn himself is a marine and although boot camp is a distant memory for him, he still has a soldier's rugged demeanor and can often be found grumbling around the place and still lifting cases of booze to his patron's car (the bar doubles as the island's only true liquor store). The joint, which gets its name from the old hats behind the bar donated by people over the years as payments for bar tabs, tends to attract a mix of expats and Viequenses who take their drink seriously. As a tourist, as long as your voice and style of dress are not too loud, you should blend in just fine. If you're hungry, the microwave hotdog creation that's available from the bartender is just about as good a late-night-snack as there ever was. The most eclectic jukebox on Vieques, a sturdy pool table, a few gambling machines and tiny used-book trading spot round out the offerings here. **B3**
787.741.2416

Kama Nightclub. Vieques isn't exactly a nightclub-style island. Which makes this club an especially nice surprise. It's got all the feeling of a chic city dance club – right down to the 1964 vintage Triumph motorcycle on display behind the bar – with absolutely none of the attitude. A local groovy jam band takes the stage many nights and they are supplemented with a rotating selection of guest DJs. Open weekends only. **B4**
787.741.8600

Esperanza

On the weekends, the young Viequenses cruise up and down the malecon (the walkway along the shore in Esperanza) with their reggaeton blasting. Because the whole stretch can be driven in under a minute, they turn around and do it again. And again!

If that's not your style, you can still have a great time cruising the joints along Esperanza's fun and funky waterfront street.

Stop in at **Duffy's Esperanza** at day's end, get a seat at the bar, listen to the ever-changing but always cool selection of satellite radio, and watch the setting Caribbean sun paint the sky the color of a perfect rum punch. The energy level at neighboring Banana's fluctuates with the crowd except on nights when their upstairs roof deck is open and a variety of live music or DJ sets gets local and gringo hips swaying to the rhythm.

And speaking of hips, you can watch several of Vieques' finest in action across the street at **La Nasa** – a decidedly Viequense hangout that has a great deck overlooking the water where the booty-shaking takes place on late Sunday afternoons. As a visitor, you'll be welcomed there as long as you don't try to impress everyone with your version of the Macarena. Actually, that might even endear you to the locals a little more!

For drinks in delightful, if sedate, settings, pay a visit to the bars at **El Quenepo** or **Tradewinds** where you can pretty much be left alone as you watch the ice melt in your drink like a northeastern winter in retreat.

It's also always worth checking out what's happening at **Inn on the Blue Horizon** in Vieques Events. They tend to have theme nights with live entertainment.

SHOP HERE NOW

Shop Here Now

Because Vieques is not visited by cruise ships, it is blessedly lacking a thriving shopping scene. You won't find Hermes Scarves or Gucci Handbags. But if you're gripped by the yen to spend, there are a few places that offer interesting, artsy, items at fair prices. As with most commerce on Vieques, the shops are split between the towns of Isabel Segunda and Esperanza.

Isabel Segunda

Shopping in this tiny town is more about function than form. Here you'll find the island's only ATM machines, post office, drug store and bank. Nevertheless, there are a few shops worth popping into if you're in town.

Caribbean Walk. Features a nice collection of locally-made jewelry and crafts at affordable prices. The perfect place to find a take-home souvenir while supporting the efforts of local artists. **S1**
787.741.7770

Blackbeard Sports. If it has to do with getting active you'll find it here – from camping gear to exercise gear. You'll also find a selection of shoes, T-shirts, caps, sunglasses, bathing suits and more. Bikes and scuba gear are available for rent as well. Also has Internet access available. See "Play Here Now." **S2**
www.blackbeardsports.com
info@blackbeardsports.com
787.741.1892

Playa Voltios. Surf central. Stocked with wave-jockey jewelry, skateboards, sunglasses, boardshorts, flip flops, snorkel gear, bikinis and whatever else you need to have fun on the beach. Rents and sells surf and body boards. Stop in at Maffle's Barbers next door to get an $8.00 haircut in an old-school setting! **S3**
787.741.7873

Siddhia Hutchinson Fine Art Design Studio and Gallery. If you want to take home a bit of the tropics on canvas,

there's no better place on Vieques to look than in this spacious gallery just up from the ferry dock. Siddhia has a chameleon-like style so you're sure to find something you'll like (maybe even a rendering of a chameleon?). The shop also carries a line of pottery designed by the artist. **S4**
www.siddhiahutchinson.com
gallery@siddhiahutchinson.com
787.741.8780

Beach Doggies. The super-creative owners of this shop take found objects and turn them into real finds for lovers of quirky one-of-a-kind *objets d'art*. Follow the signs directly uphill (to the south) of the ferry terminal. **S5**

Lydias. Pretty much the only place on the island to buy gift wrap and greeting cards. Also has a small selection of Vieques T-shirts and gifts. **S6**

Esperanza

Tradewinds Gift Shop. *If Found, Fill With Rum. Work Is For People Who Don't Know How To Plunder. I Don't Need A Boat To Drink Like A Sailor.* There's no better place to shop if you want to take home a well-made piece of T-shirt wisdom than this cute shop located beneath the Tradewinds restaurant. Rum-spun island sayings and artistically-designed Vieques logos bedeck caps, tank tops, muscle shirts, polo shirts and, of course, T-shirts. Other offerings here include sunglasses, whimsical jewelry, bohemian beachwear for women, dry bags, and more. **R20**

Vieques Flower and Gifts Too! Stepping into this shop is a bit like stepping into a pirate's locker. Hand-carved santos (saints) share precious shelf space with imported Buddhas, picture frames, greeting cards, and more. And even though the space is small, this shop is one of the biggest purveyors of artisan handicrafts including glass wind chimes, keychains, hand-made pottery and the mesmerizing paper mache masks known as Viagantes. For more practical needs you can also find sunscreen, disposable cameras, sunglasses, flip flops, and more. There's even a well-stocked ice cream cooler and

selection of snacks for emergency refueling while strolling the malecon. **S7**
787.741.4197

Diva's Closet. As the name might imply, this spacious boutique specializes in higher-end women's clothes. The racks are awash in linen and gauze in a variety of styles, bright beachy colors, and patterns. Bathing suits, sarongs, shirt and pant sets, cover-ups, and flip flops are all on offer with price tags to make any Diva feel at home. There is also a multihued treasure trove of jewelry available at the front counter. **S8**
787.741.7595

The Vieques Conservation and Historical Trust Gift Shop. The best reason to visit the gift shop at this conservation-oriented establishment is because they have the finest selection of eco-themed books on and about Vieques. They also have an assortment of stuffed animals, puzzles, notecards and a wonderful wall of made-in-Vieques items including glassware, pottery, platters, and carved cassava gourd art. But, if all of those reasons weren't enough to make you visit, it's good to know that every penny the shop makes goes to help support the good work of the Trust. *(For more about the Trust, see "More Here Now").* **S9**
www.vcht.com
787.741.8850

Beading Bikini. You might have to hunt around for this "Jeep Boutique"" but your efforts will be well-rewarded. In addition to being one of the island's yoga gurus, Jennifer also makes beautiful beaded jewelry from the delightfully simple to designs so dazzlingly complex that only the fingers of a yoga master could have produced them. Jenn runs her shop out of her signature blue Jeep, which you can often find parked outside of Duffy's Esperanza.
787.435.6850

Kim's Cabin. Set back a few yards in a grove off the hustle and bustle of the Malecon, this shop feels like a trading post where you might just bump into the Skipper, Maryann or Mrs. Howell. And how lucky the castaways would have been to be able to shop here and take advantage of the eclectic

selection of high-quality men's and women's clothing as well as unique jewelry, teva sandals, and more. **$10**
787.741.3145

Colmados

Colmados are the island version of general stores. They are small shops, crammed full of various items and act as part pharmacy, part department store, part liquor store, part pet shop and part grocery. They're full of personality, but not necessarily the items you are looking for, so a stop in a few of them might be necessary before you bag your quarry. Colmados are also part watering hole where you'll usually find a few friendly locals enjoying not just a few Medallas.

La Tienda Verde. Don't think "green grocer" when you think of this colmado. The "verde" in its name comes not from what's inside, but from what's outside – namely, a generous application of bright green paint that makes this reliable shop easy to spot on your way headed east of Esperanza. That's not to say it's not worth a look inside. You'll find a surprising assortment of gourmet items like olives, cheeses and pates; a selection of wines, beer and liquor; a coffee machine that turns out a decent java fix; and the usual assortment of snacks, basic household supplies, soft drinks, and cigarettes. Fresh baked bread is brought in daily and kept warm under heat lamps. The Green Store is an institution and meeting place for all on Vieques. **C1**

El Encanto. Islanders refer to this place as CBS which stands for the "Coldest Beer Store." That it does have thanks to deep chest freezers loaded up with an assortment of suds. Encanto also features a good selection of picnic supplies and snacks. In the front corner of the store a small bar does a brisk business all day long. **C2**

Colmado Mambo. *Apple sauce, anti-perspirant, aspirin. Beer, baby food, batteries. Chorizo, coffee, candy.* Getting the picture yet? Mambo has the A to Z of what you need. In fact, you'd be hard pressed to find a more efficient use of shelf space anywhere in Puerto Rico. The aisles may be narrow, but as you wind through them you'll discover true treasures on a little island like Vieques such as kalamata olives, imported mustards, Haagen Dazs ice cream, plus frozen shrimp, calamari and whole turkeys. Mambo is also part casino/bar due to its collection of slot machines on the front porch that attract an assortment of friendly islanders who enjoy sipping Medallas while flirting with Lady Luck. **C3**

Colmado Molino – This shop goes by the name of "The 11 O' Clock Store" because of its nightly closing time. This makes it the perfect place to grab a late-night pack of smokes or something to satisfy those midnight munchy attacks. **C4**

Other Markets

Supermarkets. There are two "supermarkets" on Vieques one located on Rte. 200 on the way into Isabel Segunda (**Superdescuentes Morales**) and the other in town itself (**Supermercado Morales**). These are basically much larger colmados and feature a more robust selection of fresh and pre-packaged foods. Both also feature onsite butchers for fresh meats and cold cuts. Remember, though, it's an island. You'll have fun with this in mind: *You can't always get what you want, but if you try sometimes, you just might find ... you get what you need!*

Fruit Truck. In most parts of the world, refrigerated tractor trailers are used to transport food. Through a display of true island ingenuity, on Vieques, one of them is used to *store* food. Slide in past the sturdy plastic straps and you'll have quite the selection of fruits, veggies and herbs to choose from. Some of it is fresh and wonderful, some of it is old and squishy, so choose wisely. Ask Mundo to carve up a coconut for you and enjoy the icy refreshing water inside. Located on 997 just before it meets 200.

Vieques Health Food. Healthy eating might not be high on your list whilst on vacation, but in addition to the usual soy-based, organic offerings, this store offers some truly yummy snacks. You'll also find a nice selection of healthy frozen burritos and pizzas, thai-style noodle cups, and an assortment of supplements that can help counteract all those calories, cocktails and color you'll be getting on holiday. Located on the left of Rte. 200 heading toward Isabel Segunda before supermarket and gas stations.
787.741.4744

Buen Provecho. Meaning "good appetite," this gourmet and fresh produce spot is run by the former chef at BBH and his wife, so you can rest assured that the offerings are top notch. Stop by and stock up on such delicacies as cheeses, smoked salmon, olives, artisan breads, meats, seafood, oils and vinegars, dry fruits, nuts, roasted tomatoes, white anchovies and anything else that would feel at home on a well-versed palate. www.buenprovechovieques.com **S1**
787.529.7316

PLAY HERE NOW

Play Here Now

The Biobay

Dinoflagellates. They may sound like something out of a bad sci-fi movie, but in fact they have the starring role in a nightly show that dazzles visitors to Vieques' Mosquito Bay – as of 2008, officially the brightest bioluminescent bay in the world according to the Guinness Book of World Records.

By venturing out in either kayaks or on an eco-friendly electric boat, you can see fish trailing bluish shooting-star-like patterns under the dark surface of the water because dinoflagellates (completely harmless microscopic organisms) glow like fireflies when disturbed. On either trip, you can jump overboard and swim in the bay where your movements will be traced by a vivid halo – perfect for making "light angels" by swirling your arms and legs.

> *Hint: While boating or kayaking, be sure to grab some water and sprinkle it on your legs. It'll make you believe fairy dust really does exisit! Also, you might want to bring along goggles for an interesting underwater effect. Be sure to wear eco-friendly bug repellent, bring a towel, change of clothes and just your credit cards and money in a zipper pocket in your bathing suit.*

Several tour operators will arrange for your visit to this truly stunning locale. Don't think "tour group" in the usual way, though. These tours tend to be fun, informative and low-key, **not** cheesy and irritating.

Blue Caribe. Offers kayaking tours of the bay.
http://www.enchanted-isle.com/bluecaribe/
787.741.2522

Abe's Snorkeling. Another quality biobay kayaking operator. www.abessnorkeling.com 787.741.2134

Island Adventures. Provides eco-friendly electric boat tours of the bay. Perfect if you're uneasy about kayaking.
www.biobay.com 787.741.0720

Other Recreation

The BioBay is pretty much must for all visitors to Vieques. But, if you have more time and a little extra energy, these operators can arrange for ways to have a few other mellow adventures both on and in the waters surrounding Vieques.

Abe's Snorkeling. In addition to nighttime kayaking trips, Abe also offers the chance for a more robust experience of the bio bay with what he calls an "All In One Bio Bay" tour. This trip last the better part of a day and includes kayaking, snorkeling, enjoying a prepared meal sometimes accompanied by Abe's ukulele playing and finally, touring the bio bay at night. Abe's Snorkeling, which is a family affair run by Abe, his son Abe Jr., and his wife April, also offers daytime kayaking and snorkeling trips to other areas of the island.
www.abesnorkeling.com
baboon@coqui.net
Phone: 787.741.2134
Cell: 787.435.6881

Vieques Sailing. When you think of that quintessential Caribbean sailor you've always imagined bumping into on a tropical island, you're thinking of Captain Bill, the one-man operator of Vieques Sailing. He knows the waters around Vieques like nobody's business and will be sure you have a smooth ride on his well-worn but completely charming sailboat. He'll even take you to the southern tip of the Bermuda Triangle if you're brave enough to give it a go. Refreshments and a surly running commentary are included in the ride.
Phone: 787.508.SAIL (7245)

Nansea Charters. When it comes to diving the waters surrounding Vieques, it's hard to do better than with this operation. The tours are well-run, fun and, most importantly, safe. The company runs two-tank boat trips as well as shore diving. They also provide full certification classes, open water referrals and "discover diving" courses. You can also arrange snorkeling trips and private charters.
www.nanseacharters.com   dgephoto1@aol.com
787.741.2390

Wildfly Charters. Captain Greg McKee's passion for fishing is evidenced by the Fish Stories series of writing he maintains on the Enchanted Isle website (see below). He'd be happy to share that passion and his considerable knowledge with you out on the water in his flats boat that does its thing by floating in less than six inches of water. He provides everything you need – including expert knowledge of where the fish hang out – to bag your tarpon, bonefish or permit fish. Greg is a true waterman, with Key West and a ride in Jimmy Buffet's plane in his recent past.
www.wildflycharters.com
gmckee1@hotmail.com
787.435.4833
Fish Stories: www.enchanted-isle.com/fishstories

Marauder Sailing. Marauder is the name a 34-foot sailing yacht that offers you the chance to sunbathe on its deck or seek shade in its covered cockpit. It's also the name of what you'll feel like after you've taken advantage of the open bar this outfit offers on both its full day and sunset sails!
787.435.4858

Black Beard Sports. Before this sports shop and outfitter arrived on Vieques, adventure sports were kind of a lose venture basically consisting of buying a tent from Walmart on the main island and finding your own patch of land on which to set it up. Black Beard has gotten things whipped up into a proper operation and now offers diving trips as well as bike and camping gear rentals. Their shop is well-equipped with everything you need to get outdoorsy and even has a business center with fax and Internet access so that you can check in with the world before you leave it behind.
www.blackbeardsports.com
info@blackbeardsports.com
787.741.1892

Vieques Adventures. Aptly named, this operation can arrange for fully-guided or self-guided explorations of Vieques on earth or the sea. Watery activities include kayak fishing and exploring trips to some of the lesser-known areas around the island. Land-based adventures consist of Mt. Biking along Vieques's lesser known trails. If you choose to

take a trip with Gary, you'll benefit from his extensive knowledge of things natural. If you choose to go it alone, he won't be offended – and will even drop off your gear at most hotels and guest houses.
www.viequesadventures.com
gary@viequesadventures.com
787.692.9162

Caribbean Fly Fishing Co. It would be easy to recommend captain Franco Gonzalez because he has the same first name as my last name. But there's even a better reason – he seems to know where all the fish are. Franco will take you out on a Ranger 21 bay boat to either the north or south side of Vieques and provide you the gear you need to succeed in hooking anything from a barracuda off the coast to a tarpon inshore.
www.caribbeanflyfishingco.com
flyfish@coqui.net
787.741.1337

Blue Caribe Kayaks. In addition to offering tours of the biobay, this laid-back outfit on the Malecon in Esperanza will also rent kayaks for your own exploration of the waters off Vieques. An easy adventure is to just carry your kayak across the street and paddle out to Cayo Afuera, the island you can see just off the coast. Snorkeling on the west side of the island can often be rewarding. Blue Caribe also offers combo tours joining a daytime snorkel trip with their evening biobay tour. Located on Malecon in Esperanza.
www.bluecaribekayaks.com
bluecaribe@caribe.net
787.741.2522

GO WILD HERE NOW

Go Wild Here Now
Natural Vieques

Fauna

Except for the horses, the fauna on Vieques tends toward the small, harmless side. That's not to say there aren't a few creepy, crawly things you might come across. But remember ... even the tarantulas, scorpions and centipedes (if you even cross paths with any of them) don't deliver anything worse than the equivalent of a wasp sting.

Coqui. If you're planning on sleeping to nothing but the sounds of the waves washing the beach or the wind clacking the palm fronds during your stay on Vieques, forget about it. The island is blessed (some peace-and-quiet seekers would say cursed) with a healthy population of coqui frogs who beep out their high-pitched ko-kee calls all night long. Give it a little time though and their sound will become as synonymous with the tropics as pina coladas and Jimmy Buffet. Otherwise, there's always the aircon or earplugs! Although they're easy to hear, coquis are exceedingly difficult to spot because of their super-small size of just ½ to 3 inches in length. They may surprise you, though, peering down from your showerhead with their large black eyes.

Tarantula. They might be scary and hairy but in reality, tarantulas aren't all that threatening. In fact, the only way you're likely to get bit by one is if you started poking your finger in one of their faces, and why would you do that? Chances are you won't even come across one unless there have been plentiful rains which forces them up from their holes in the ground. But before you think about squashing one, keep in mind that female tarantulas have been known to live to be 30-40 years old. And, let's not forget – they eat other bugs. Much better to try to sweep one of these significant creatures out with a broom than to give it the shoe treatment!

Scorpion. The word alone is enough to send shivers down spines – never mind the curled tail that always seems hungry for something to inject. But don't be alarmed, on Vieques, your imagination's take on a scorpion is probably much bigger than the actual creature. On Vieques, these arachnids (yes, they are in the same class as spiders) are tiny, ranging from about two to six inches in total length. They are nocturnal and like to hide in dark corners, so again, no poking! But if you do have the rare bad luck of getting bit by one, it's nothing that an ice cube and shot of tequila couldn't take care of. Ice goes on the sore spot, tequila goes down the hatch. And just think of the story you'll have to tell!

Gecko. Chances are good you'll get surprised by one of these little lizards racing across a wall in your hotel room or at a restaurant. Fear not, they are completely harmless and do a good job of keeping mosquitoes at bay. And, maybe because they can't out-shout the coquis, these geckos don't produce that high-pitched squeaking sound that their brethren make in other places around the world.

Mongoose. Another surprising sight, these furry brown ferret-like creatures dart across the roads of Vieques all day long. In one of those "what were they thinking?" moments of planning, the story goes that mongooses were introduced to the island to take care of the rats. Problem is that rats are nocturnal and – you guessed it – mongooses are diurnal (and yes, you really do say "mongooses"). Now they both live in harmony, but odds are you'll only come across the mongoose during your stay, not their intended prey.

Iguana. Although they can reach lengths of up to seven-feet long, most of the iguanas on Vieques are of the small variety and hang out in a few favorite trees around the island. If you want to spot one, you can check the tree next door to Al's Mar Azul. While they might appear sluggish, if you see one darting out of the way of a car on the road, you'll be surprised out how fast the dinosaur-looking creatures can really move. While they're completely at home on Vieques now, they're not really a native species. They were brought here by early settlers as pets who then set them loose when they got bored with them.

Centipede. When people talk about the "C" word on Vieques, these little nasties are what they're referring to. Resembling long red worms, centipedes don't look too menacing, but, in fact, their bite is the worst on the island

and, if not treated, can lead to some pretty serious infection. Again though, sighting one is pretty rare. There are people who've lived on the island for years and only come across the million-leggers one or two times and even then, were easily able to avoid a bite. Just don't go routing around in old wood piles and you should be fine!

Horses. There are two types of horses on Vieques. The first, the wild horse, you'll spot practically everywhere, although two of the most beautiful spots to see them is at Sun Bay or in the area of the island where the old Navy bunkers are. The joke about these beautiful beasts is that if one is eating the flower bed in your neighbor's garden, then he's a wild horse. If you try to put a saddle on one, then that horse's owner will appear really fast! Whether that's true or not, it doesn't really matter. The wild horses on Vieques are as much a part of the island as its beaches and the salsa music that blares from La Nasa on Sundays. They're sure to take up a good amount of space on your digital picture card!

The other type of horses you may encounter on Vieques are the Paso Finos. You'll know one of these when you see a proud young Viequense trotting by and you hear the horse's distinctive one-two-three-four clopping. Unlike other horses that move their legs two-at-a-time, Paso Finos move each one independently giving their mounts an incredibly smooth ride. Paso Finos are the first horse to appear in the Americas (after early horses were wiped out by the ice age), and are the result of a trio of equines brought to the New World by Columbus. Once ridden by Spanish Conquistadors, they are now ridden in competitions around the world as well as, of course, along the streets of Vieques.

Other Natural Attractions

Ceiba Tree. The ceiba (pronounced say-bah) is the national tree of Puerto Rico – and Vieques has a beautiful example of one sitting by itself in a field on the way to Green Beach. The roots are like low walls creating tiny nooks and crannies from which it's possible to take some great snapshots. In ancient Mayan civilizations, it was believed that a ceiba tree was at the center of the world, connecting earth to heaven. When you see this three- to four-hundred year old beauty, you'll know why. Located on Rte. 200 on the right at the base of short hill, before ferry dock when heading to Green Beach.

Laugna Kiani. Also on the way to Green Beach, this small park features a series of boardwalks that lead you through mangroves to a serene lagoon where you can do some good birdwatching. Try to spot the crabs down in the mud on either side of the walkway as you head out. And don't forget to apply mosquito repellent. Lots. Open from 6AM to 6PM.

MORE HERE NOW

More Here Now
Other Attractions

The Bunkers. During the years of the Navy's occupation of Vieques, munitions and other military-oriented paraphernalia was stored in a series of bunkers located on the eastern end of the island. Today, these bunkers are abandoned but the area of the island in which they lie makes for a great drive and an even better bike ride or jog. The roads are narrow, but in pretty good repair and they wind through acres of beautiful countryside at the base of Monte Pirata, the highest mountain on Vieques. Occasionally you'll find one of the bunker doors unlocked. Don't be afraid to hop in and give a hoot or holler. They make exceptional echo chambers! See island maps for location.

El Fortín Conde de Mirasol. This impressive structure located on a hill above Isabel Segunda was originally built in 1845 and is the last fort built by the Spanish in the Caribbean. It took over ten years and thousands of dollars to complete, leading Queen Isabele of Spain to famously ask if the walls were made of gold. The fort sat empty for many years before being restored and turned into the museum it is now that has a collection of Taino Indian and other earlier artifacts as well as informative exhibits that tell of the island's history. Open Wednesday through Sunday from 10AM to 4PM. See Isabel Segunda map for location.
787.741.1717

The Vieques Conservation and Historical Trust. There's truly no better place on Vieques to learn about its wild side than at this museum/educational center located in the center of the Esperanza strip. According to their mission statement, the goal of this hard-working organization is to *protect the unique archeological, physical and ecological environment existing on Vieques.* Paramount among their work is striving to preserve Vieques' stunning bioluminescent bay. The center has hands-on salt-water tanks; exhibits, movies and presentations that instruct about the island's history, flora and fauna; and a museum featuring rotating shows. There is also a small computer room that offers Internet access for $3.00 per half hour and a great gift shop whose proceeds

benefit the trust. Open Tuesday – Sunday from 11AM to 4PM. On malecon in Esperanza. www.vcht.com
787.741.8850

Faro Punta Mulas, The Lighthouse. Originally built in 1895 and restored in 1992 this iconic lighthouse is worth a visit if for no other reason that to soak up a bit of peace and quiet in the madness that Isabel Segunda can sometimes be. From here you can watch the ferry come and go, let your gaze sail out to the main island of Puerto Rico as well as Culebra and on out to St. John and St. Thomas on really clear days. Allegedly the beam from the lighthouse could actually be seen on those faraway Virgin Islands. There is a small maritime museum in the lighthouse building but there seems to be no plans to reopen it or allow access to the lighthouse directly. Entrance to the grounds, therefore, is free. See Isabel Segunda map.

La Capilla Ecuménica. This picturesque chapel on the right side of the road as you head to Green Beach may be small, but it has a big history. It was originally built on the big island of Puerto Rico to commemorate a chapel that was destroyed by authorities on Vieques during the protest years. In 2003, the governor of Puerto Rico decided to send the church back to Vieques but he sent it to Isabel Segunda via barge. Of course, the church was too big to drive through the streets of Isabel II, so eventually another barge was sent and it was relocated to its current spot. Now, it is an oasis of peace that serves as a memorial to turbulent times.

The Vieques Humane Society. It might seem odd to put this on a list of attractions in a tourism book, but stopping by this hard-working organization and taking a "sato" (the island name that basically means "mutt") out for a much needed walk or day on the beach could just turn into the highlight of your trip! The Society is in desperate need of funds, donations, and volunteers to help them deal with the never-ending problem of stray animal care. And, what better souvenir to take home than a living, breathing one that will shower you with unconditional love forever! Open 10am-2pm Tues, Fri, Sat. See Isabel Segunda map.
www.viequeshs.org
787.741.0209

KNOW HERE NOW

Know Here Now
Practicalities

Note: All phone numbers begin with 787-741 unless otherwise noted.

ATM. You can get cash at the ATM machine located at Banco Popular on the main street in Isabel Segunda (see map). All major electronic teller services work at the machine.

Car Rental Companies. A car rental is pretty much a MUST for a successful vacation on Vieques. The island does have several "publicos" or taxi-vans but they are largely unreliable and useful really only to take you from the ferry dock or airport to your hotel or car rental company. The island can run out of rentals so you are advised to book early.

> **Island**: 1666
> **Maritza:** 0078
> **Martineau:** 0087
> **Chepito's:** 8691
> **Marcos:** 1388
> **Steve's:** 8135
> **Vieques:** 1037

Cell phones. As of this writing, all cell phones work on the island except Nextel.

Churches. Religious life on the island is decidedly Christian with the following offerings:

> **Catholic.** Parroquia Immaculada Concepcion, Isabel Segunda. Saturdays 7PM/Sundays 11AM. 2241.
>
> **Episcopal.** Todos Los Santos Epsicopal Church, Isabel Segunda. Sundays 9AM. 2668.
>
> **Methodist.** Esperanza. Sunday 10AM, Tuesday 7PM. 8520.

Church of Jesus Christ of Latter Day Saints. Isabel Segunda, near the ferry dock. Sundays 10AM. 787.553.4440

Driving. The roads on Vieques are, for the most part, in good shape. However, in many places, they get quite narrow and, in order for two cars to pass each other, a bit of finesse is called for. Of course, you can't always count on islanders for on-the-spot courtesy so you really do need to stay alert and be ready to jerk the car off to the side of the road at any moment. Throw in the odd cow, horse, or iguana and things get really interesting! Just get yourself in an island frame of mind and take it slow *hombre*. There are no traffic lights on the island.

Gas Station. There are two gas stations that are reliably open and they are pretty much across the street from each other on the airport road (Rte. 200) heading toward Isabel Segunda. Occasionally, the island does run out of gas, so make sure you keep the tank topped up.

Laundry. The only laundromat on the island is located in Isabel Segunda, just across the street from Al's Mar Azul.

Medical Care. Vieques does have a hospital that can handle some emergencies and at least stabilize patients before having them airlifted to the main island. There are also two doctors and two dentists on the island as well as a (usually) well-stocked pharmacy. (Hint: if you need a prescription filled or refilled, you are allowed to cut the mammoth queue in the pharmacy because you will be paying cash. Just go right up the window and conduct your business.). Viequenses don't really believe in making doctor appointments so if you need medical care for anything other than an emergency, just show up and wait. For a long, long, time.

    Hospital: 3282
    Dr. Jose Figueroa: 2222
    Dr. Luis Rivera: 0738
    Dra. Fanny Garraton (dentist): 8765
    Dr. Juan Ramos (dentist): 8887

Imagen Optica (eye care): 4969
Pharmacia San Antonio (Isabel Segunda): 8397

Language. You'll be able to get by just fine with English, as all locals study it in school and have at least some proficiency with it. If you do speak a little Spanish, you'll stand a better chance of getting to know some Viequense residents. However, be warned: the style of Spanish spoken on Vieques is mysteriously missing the letter "s." So "gracias" becomes "gracia" and "como estas" becomes "como eta." Once your ear adjusts you'll get the hang of it and, if you speak the same way, you'll be more like a local and less like a tourist with every "do [never *dos*] cerveza (two beers) you order.

Pampering and Fitness. While there are no spas on Vieques (until the W opens in April), there are several massage therapists and yoga instructors who would be happy to schedule sessions with you at a location of your choice. Daily Yoga classes are held at Hix Island House (see "Stay Here Now") and on the beach – check Vieques Events (see below) for most up-to-date schedule. There is one public gym on the island but the process needed to get a pass is pretty much a defeating workout in and of itself. It is located on the square in Isabel Segunda (ask at the tourism office). Occasional on-demand spin classes are held at Utopia Fitness, located at Enchanted Garden (see "Stay Here Now").

Massage Therapists/Yoga Instructors

Angeles Massage and Yoga: 1378
Aldo Robert: 787.206.9582
Blue Hoku Yoga and Massage (Maureen): 787.988.8622
Carol Thompson (Trager): 787.314.6951
Christine Holgers: 787.435.1313
Ingrid Bergman: 787.435.1313
John Duffany: 0341
Bien Herrera: 787.406.7394
Georgia Pine: 4837
Sea Rhydr: 787.556.7511
Spirit Within: (Reiki): 787.616.5309

Publicos. See "car rental companies" above. If you do want to try your luck with publicos, here are a few numbers that may or may not get you results:

> **Ana Robles:** 2318
> **Eric:** 0448
> **Fernando:** 787.605.4100
> **Henry:** 8621
> **Ismael:** 0095
> **Jorge:** 2116
> **Josue:** 787.366.7392
> **Jose Morales:** 787.435.4277
> **Julian:** 787.385.7604
> **Luis Gonazales:** 7768

Safety. While person-to-person violent crime is virtually nonexistent on Vieques, petty theft does occur, especially on the beaches. You are advised not to take valuables to the beach or to leave them in your car. Thieves sometimes hide in the brush backing the shoreline and wait until you are swimming to run out and hoist your bag. It is also advisable to leave the windows of your rental car open when you go to the beach to avoid the headache of a curious thief smashing a window to see what's inside. All that being said, Vieques remains relatively safe and thousands of tourists have wonderful vacations on the island each year without any incident whatsoever.

> **Police:** 2020
> **Fire:** 1616
> **US Fish and Wildlife:** 2138

Side Trip. Guests who are visiting Vieques for more than a few days often wonder if it is worth taking a side trip to the nearby island of Culebra. In short, the answer is "no." The amount of money, time and effort required to first go back to the main island and then get over to Culebra is simply not a good idea. If you want to see Culebra, it would be more advisable to relocate there after a few days on Vieques. Culebra's got one stunner of a beach (Playa Flamingo) but beyond that, tends to offer much less than Vieques which is truly is the star of the Spanish Virgin Islands.

Tourism Office (0800). The island's tourism office is located off the square in Isabel Segunda, but they won't be able to tell you much more than this book!

WiFi. Your hotel will likely offer wireless Internet but if the service is out, you can bring your laptop to Roy's Coffee Lounge where you can surf and sip at the same time. If you didn't bring a laptop, you can hop on a computer at the The Vieques Conservation and Historical Trust for a very reasonable fee.

Resources

Vieques Events. While every attempt is made to keep this guidebook 100% up-to-date, things can change quickly on the island. For the most current information on news and events, this publication can't be beat. You can download new issues every month at www.viequesevents.net.

Other Helpful Websites:
www.enchanted-isle.com
www.viequesvisitor.com

Further Reading. The book, *Vieques, A Photographically Illustrated Guide to the Island, Its History and Its Culture* offers a wonderful history of the island with lots of high-quality photos. It makes great reading before you go and a nice souvenir to have when you return home. It can be ordered on Amazon or at:

http://www.stjohnbeachguide.com/Vieques_HTML/Vieques_English.htm

Notes

Notes

Notes

Notes

Notes

Notes

Notes

Notes

Notes

Notes

Notes

Notes

Made in the USA